I LOVE THE BOOK. It brought back nothing but good, happy memories of a happy childhood. . . You have shared with the world how childhood needn't be filled with expensive toys to be some of the happiest memories of your life.
Joaan Nemyer Desvousges,
Bessemer, AL
WBHS, '66

I found myself looking forward to the times that I could spend getting away from my day-to-day work related responsibilities to tag along with you as you shared your experiences in this wonderfully structured guided tour of the Boom Times.
Rene', Naert, PhD.
Alliant International University
San Diego, CA
OLR '62, WBHS'67

Brockman has hit the high notes for baby boomers, from family dinners to long forgotten TV shows. His relationship with Michigan's nature is a great touch! If you are a boomer, open a Faygo pop, sit back and enjoy.
George Emanoil, President, Questech, Inc.
Farmington Hills, MI
WLHS, '68

Growing Up In
Boom Times

Chris Brockman

authorHOUSE®

AuthorHouse™
1663 Liberty Drive
Bloomington, IN 47403
www.authorhouse.com
Phone: 1-800-839-8640

First published by AuthorHouse   5/31/2011

ISBN: 978-1-4567-6830-0 (sc)
ISBN: 978-1-4567-6829-4 (hc)
ISBN: 978-1-4567-6828-7 (e)

Library of Congress Control Number: 2011907441

Printed in the United States of America

Any people depicted in stock imagery provided by Thinkstock are models, and such images are being used for illustrative purposes only. Certain stock imagery © Thinkstock.

This book is printed on acid-free paper.

This book is dedicated to Julie, my partner on life's journey, who helps me make new memories every day.

Those were such happy times
And not so long ago.
How I wondered where they'd gone. . .

The Carpenters
Yesterday Once More

INTRODUCTION

"(Beep) What's (beep) your (beep) name? (beep)"
"(Beep) Jackie. (beep)"
"(Beep) How (beep) old (beep) are (beep) you? (beep)"
"(Beep) Twelve. (beep)"
"(Beep) Call (beep) me. (Beep) My (beep) number (beep) is... (beep)"

We might have called it "Our Space." It might have been a big deal if the media had been tracking and broadcasting every single thing adolescents did with electronic devices. Instead, it was 1960, and we called it "The Pipeline." Kids used it as an underground way of making contact. It was primitive by today's standards, but in its own crude way it provided us kids with a way to communicate with other kids.

Someone had figured out that dialing a certain number connected callers to the same busy signal, and they could talk to each other between the beeps. On a slow summer day, my buddies and I might spend a couple of hours giving and getting phone numbers and meeting girls. It wasn't much, but it signified a need and an inventiveness that has always characterized us Baby Boomers.

We are the most celebrated generation ever. We have skewed every statistic and slice of life it represents. In the process, we have changed, and we have changed the world. It isn't as if we invented change. 2,500 years ago, Heraclitus made his observation that all things are in the state of flux, to which someone doubtless replied, "Well yeah, duh."

The pace and significance of change, however, have accelerated greatly in our lifetimes. Everything has gotten bigger, faster, more complicated, and less personal. We have become wealthier, our possessions have increased dramatically, our standard of living has risen. We are living longer. Yet we are also working more hours, and we never seem to have time to enjoy our possessions, nor do we seem ever to be satisfied. Our dwellings have ballooned and our personal space has expanded, but we spend much more time eating fast food and less and less time at the family dinner table talking to one another. Our children start school in diapers and are technology savvy almost before they can talk, but much of their time in front of screens is taken up with playing games or writing virtual notes.

We Boomers like to think we have ever greater control over our lives, and in many ways we do. We expect this comes from our research and creativity, and the technology and new products we have created. At the same time, our landfills are bourgeoning with the products we continually discard in favor of the latest versions. The gross domestic product, gross executive salaries, and the tax revenue they generate depend upon consumer spending in overdrive. If we don't continually buy more stuff we don't need, we're told, our lifestyle and the economy will go to hell. Our *lifestyle* has caused a gross increase in obesity and diabetes, which negate some of the medical advances we have made.

Many of the advances in medicine, as well as much of the skyrocketing costs, are in new wonder drugs. Some of these have proven to be unnecessary, ineffectual, or even harmful. The biggest advance in medicine may be the exponential growth of the insurance industry, which contributes nothing to good health, but voraciously sucks up health care dollars.

Things have changed greatly since 1946, since we were kids, since we were adolescents. The underlying intent of *Boom Times* is to renew both your sense of wonder and your sense of responsibility about change by reminding you of the way things used to be. I have tried not to not be didactic or preachy in accomplishing this, and I have tried to be reasonably objective in my overall attitude toward change.

I do, however, have a strong tendency towards nostalgia. I enjoy remembering, and I celebrate the life that was mine that fit into the times that were ours. This doesn't mean that I would go back to everything as it was. I would never go back to using a typewriter! I welcome change.

Change is life. But, all change is not created equal, and all change is surely not good or as good as it should be.

The second major purpose of *Boom Times* is to be entertaining. More particularly, I hope it will result in your entertaining yourself. My childhood is not yours; my memories are not yours. I believe, however, that as members of a very significant and identifiable generation, we share many of the same sorts of memories from similar types of childhood experiences. If you find it as interesting and rewarding to visit the past a bit as I have, my second purpose will be fulfilled. My "research" has put me into closer touch with three generations of family, as well as with old friends. It also has put me into closer touch with myself, through the part of me shaped by the past.

I have addressed this so far to other Baby Boomers. Its message is equally important to younger people. Despite the fact that I think that change is too often pushed on us by the large, powerful forces in our society, I also think that in our free society we individuals have the ultimate power to direct change in the direction we think is best. Younger generations have or will have an increasingly important role in deciding how our society will change. My own adult children aver that things have already changed greatly since they were children, and I can only imagine the changes my grandchildren will see. It's up to them, and it's up to you to change our lives and our world for the better.

Chris Brockman
May 1, 2011

CHAPTER ONE

Home Place

It was kind of like the Beverly Hillbillies in reverse. My parents hadn't struck it rich, they weren't hopelessly unsophisticated, they didn't move with their adult children and granny, and heaven knows they didn't move into a mansion. They also didn't have a "*see*ment" pond; they had a cement floor instead.

The cement floor was in what would eventually become our dining room. It was the entrance room to the house, and in a curious concession to aesthetics, the floor was studded with marbles that had been planted in the wet cement. It became one of the pastimes of my very early life to try to get those marbles out of the floor.

Where I live now, in North Carolina, people call the house where they grew up their "home place." My parents' home places were in small town USA-- Miamisburg, Ohio. Both had moved there at about the same time, as six year olds. My dad's family moved from an even smaller Ohio town, St. Henry, so my grandfather could seek his fortune working in a mill, in walking distance up the railroad tracks from their Third St. house. My mother came directly from the family farm near Franklin, after her own mother died from tuberculosis. The expense of taking care of his consumptive young wife had cost my grandfather the farm, so he moved his family to Fourth and Buckeye and went to work in the factory, at Frigidaire in Dayton.

Though my parents were in the same high school class and lived only

1

five blocks apart, they had nothing to do with each other in high school. My mother was the attractive, popular drum majorette for the band. My dad worked in a grocery store after school. Fortunately, my dad was good looking enough to catch my mom's eye after they graduated. There's a picture of him with his wavy hair, in dark glasses and white tee shirt, leaning full length against his black '40 Mercury. (Did James Dean steal my dad's look?) They got married while my dad was home on a two-week's leave between trips with the Merchant Marine. He didn't see his three month-old baby, my sister, until he got home a year later.

When my dad returned from his service in World War II, he went to work at "the Cash," (National Cash Register) in Dayton. My mother had worked there during the war in a "high-tech" job, as a comptometer operator. They bought a cottage in Ellerton, across the Great Miami River and upstream from Miamisburg. The cottage was quaint and in a country setting, but maybe just a tad too much so. The arrangements featured an outhouse and a hand pump for water in the back yard. This was "a little hard," my dad admits, on my mother, especially with one small child and another on the way.

Because my dad hated working in the factory, it was easy for one of his friends, who had taken up painting houses, to talk him into going to work with him. This gave him a trade he could pursue anywhere. Then, another couple he and my mother knew told them about a wonderful resort-like area they had found in Oakland County Michigan. My parents visited the area, loved it, and bought a "vacation home" and two lots in a subdivision on beautiful Middle Straits Lake, for $2,500. With their not yet one year-old son and their three year-old daughter, my folks packed everything they owned into a borrowed stake truck and headed north. I had a home place.

***

Oakland County Michigan has over 450 named, clear glacial lakes and a bunch of others waiting to become the center of a subdivision.. What my parents bought on aptly named Woodview Ave. was a part of the dream of residents of the nearby urban areas of metropolitan Detroit to get out of the scorching city in the summer and to the woods and water of Oakland County. Summer cottages had sprung up around many of the lakes, and eventually subdivisions were laid out. Our subdivision was and still is called the Riding Club Subdivision. Whether this was actually descriptive at one time or merely wishful thinking, I don't know, but there wasn't a whole lot of riding (with the exception of bicycles) going on in the fifteen years I lived there.

Among the covenants in the charter for the Riding Club Subdivision (I discovered many years later) was one that prohibited the sale of property to "Negroes and Jews." Apparently this was a standard provision outside of the city, and in this case, way outside of the South. When I discovered this, long after my family had moved from there, and showed it to my parents, they were surprised, but far from incredulous. Whether it was from provisions such as this one, or a host of other reasons, I and most everyone else outside of Michigan's bigger cities grew up in lily-white neighborhoods. Virtually the only African Americans I saw in the flesh, prior to going to college, were in Pontiac, in Detroit, or were porters on the trains we took several times back to Ohio. There also were never any Jewish families in our neighborhood. Since I went to a Catholic primary school, I also had zero contact with any Jewish kids there, though I sincerely doubt it would have been very much different in the local public schools.

Our new home place featured a beautiful lake with a fine sandy beach for residents of the subdivision. The subdivision was maybe half built up, with a mix of summer cottages and year-round homes and with denser development closer to the lake. Our house was near the back corner farthest from the highway, about a quarter of a mile from the lake and the beach and with woods close on two sides. The woods and the lake would be my constant playground for the next fifteen years. The house would be my dad's and my mom's home-improvement project for much of the same time.

It started on day one. Indoor "facilities," it seemed, were not a necessity for a summer cottage, here in paradise. They were an *absolute* necessity, my mother insisted, for any home that she was going to *stay* in. My dad got the message, and as fast as you can say "indoor plumbing," he had added on a space to one end of the house for a utility room and a bathroom with a basic toilet and shower. That took care of the *indoor* part, for the time being.

As every *experienced* plumber knows, however, there's an outside part as well. Since my dad had grown up in the city and his only other house had had an outdoor privy, his experience with sewage systems was limited to nothing. Before he was done creating a working septic system, he would be a whole lot more knowledgeable, and his knowledge would be a whole lot more up close and personal. For now, he simply tied into the existing drainage system.

In a few years, the existing drainage system was found to be lacking. This was fairly easy to conclude from the fact that the drains and the toilet began backing up on one end. On the other, the ground on one end of our property began to mimic the proverbial pig sty. My dad persuaded my newly-minted uncle Dean to come up from Ohio to help him with "engineering" a new drainage system. I'm sure there was some mention of the great fishing in the lake, because my Uncle Dean was an avid hunter and fisherman. It's a good thing he brought his waders.

Together, they spent a week hand digging a hole in the rock-hard clay for a septic tank, and then trenches for a drainage field. I can specifically remember my uncle, in his waders, standing in a hole close to the house and shoveling out some foul-smelling black stuff from our "grease trap." Next thing I knew, we had a bona fide septic tank and were wise in the ways they do things in the country. My dad remodeled the bathroom and added a tub. A few years later we had a man with a bulldozer come to extend the drainage field, and "just like that" we had a 20th century bathroom and fully functional sewage system.

While the bulldozer guy was there, my dad asked him to dig up the rock that was sticking up just a bit in our dirt driveway. "No problem," said our savvy civil engineer, "I'll just..." The next think you know, our humble driveway gave birth to a monster rock, a solid rectangle about seven feet long and three feet square. My parents had bulldozer guy push down to the back edge of our property, where it oversaw our "leaf pile" until we moved years later. I don't know why they didn't have it moved to the front yard where it would have made a to-die-for lawn ornament. I guess we all thought of it as just a big old rock at the time.

***

It doesn't seem as if many people still buy fixer-uppers and spend years improving them. There ought to be a lot more experienced homes around than ever to work on, but with all the new developments of bigger and bigger houses, it appears that almost everyone wants a brand new house with all the amenities these days. In the 1950's, serial remodeling and additions to houses were popular ways for people to invest their time and money. In my neighborhood, people were always working on their own houses, creating sweat equity. It could be that this was because there were so many tradespeople who lived there. It was definitely a working class neighborhood, with lots of carpenters, plumbers, painters, roofers, and landscapers. The predominance of home improvement was also due to the fact that so many of the houses *needed* work done on them. Our own house was a continuous, slow-moving repair and construction zone.

Many home improvement projects in my neighborhood were undertaken simply to provide the basics. Others were for new extravagances such as rec rooms or a second bathroom. Often the line between necessity and luxury was blurred. We, for example, had an oil-burning space heater in the living room. Central heating in Michigan certainly provided a superior level of comfort, but a furnace for us would have to wait. In truth, the space heater was great for bellying up to on frigid nights. Roughhousing with my sister guaranteed, though, that I would have memories of more than once burning myself on that stove.

One advantage of having a very small house was that the space heater generally did keep us warm, as long as we didn't close the bedroom doors. This was true at least for my sister and me, who shared a tiny bedroom off one end of the living room. I'm not sure how true it was for my parents. Their bedroom was behind the living room, with no direct opening into it.

In the living room, we also had a fireplace that was cheery and of great utility for roasting hot dogs and toasting marshmallows. I don't think we ever used it to pop corn, but I remember eating popcorn in front of a roaring fire any number of times (maybe because we made popcorn so often!). I also can picture my sisters and me, for whatever reason, in front of the flames eating grilled cheese sandwiches and tomato soup, also staples. Most of the time, however, it had a painted-gray piece of plywood in front of it to keep the air in the house from escaping.

As a heating device, the fireplace probably resulted in a net *loss* of heat. One thing we never lacked, however, was plenty of good firewood to feed it. Our lots had giant oak and maple trees on them, which needed to be thinned. Conveniently, my Uncle John, who lived in the same neighborhood, had a tree and landscape service. Several times he came over with his crew and put on a sensory show, complete with the snarl of chainsaws, the acrid smell of oil and gas and exhaust mixed with the sweet smell of new-cut wood, and the flash of white wood chips showering from the cut. Cut into 20" logs, the felled trees provided us kids a woodpile to climb on, a home for several snakes, plenty of splitting exercise for my dad, and a continuing supply of wood to feed the fireplace.

Gruff and growly, Uncle John was a lot like one of his big McCullough chainsaws. He was blocky and powerful, building on the frame of the fullback he'd been in high school. Each Popeye forearm carried a tattoo he'd gotten in the service, artistically rendered to emphasize the muscles underneath. There was high drama when my lumberjack uncle scaled a tree to rope it off and his men pulled on the ropes to get it to fall just right. The sputtering saw would explode and chew into the tree, spitting out the stream of fragrant chips. Then, there'd be a loud splintering "Crack!" and a great uptake of air by the spectators, and the tree would whoosh to the ground with a mighty crash, always landing exactly where it was supposed to.

My uncle came around, as well, twice a year to spray for mosquitoes, of which we otherwise had swarms. One of his crew pulled a tank and compressor on wheels behind his truck, across the property, while Uncle John sprayed with a firehose up into the trees, until they dripped, with DDT. His sole concession to safety was a red bandanna over his nose and mouth. He certainly didn't wear a respirator. We kids would stand out watching him—it was another good show.

Against the frigid Michigan winters, the ceiling insulation in our house was minimal, and there probably was no insulation in the walls. The winters would produce an abundance of snow, and on sunny days it would melt off our roof. There were no gutters in the back of the house, so the most colossal icicles would grow from the edge of the roof, sometimes all the way down to the ground, if we kids didn't knock them down first. Target practice at icicles with hard-packed snowballs was great fun and a good service too. An alternative use of icicles was to suck on them, like a Popsicle. Sparkling diamond-like in the sun they looked mighty good. Presumably, all the DDT had washed off the roof by this time.

***

When my parents were able to afford a furnace, there was already a space for it in the utility room, which had been added on to the original cottage, to the outside of my parents' bedroom. This was evidenced by the double-hung window between them. The utility room is where we kept the ringer washing machine. Despite my mother's admonitions, we kids had a lot of fun rolling our hands and forearms into the rubber-covered rollers of the wringer. We only stopped when my little sister got her arm in past the elbow and couldn't get it back out, resulting in a pretty flat arm and some very scared kids. I truly don't remember (guilty consciences have a way of expunging information), but I *suspect* that my little sister didn't come up with the idea of putting her arm in the wringer all by herself.

The job of running the ductwork for the furnace fell to my father, of course. Except for that cement floor in the front, the house was on a two-foot crawlspace. My dad had to wiggle his way around on his back under the house, working overhead to anchor the ducts to the floor joists. There was more than once, he likes to tell, that he would turn and look into the beady eyes of a rat. At least it was a country rat.

***

We originally shared water with the house behind us. Two brothers lived there, one my older sister's age and one mine. My sister would have nothing to do with the older boy, Jimmy, but Timmy and I were frequent companions. We also were just as frequently adversaries. Our favorite pastime was throwing either dirtballs or stones at things, or at each other. I don't know if it was because she knew that Timmy was a much better shot than I was, but when I ended up with a gash in my forehead from a Timmy-thrown stone, my mother strongly discouraged me from playing with him anymore. There was at least one other time I received this suggestion. It was when Jimmy and Timmy made up a little song about me and a neighbor girl, which was obviously supposed to be an insult. So, I asked my mom, "What does "Chris and Connie sitting in a tree/F-*-*-*-I-N-G" mean." She never told me what it meant, but she did say that I shouldn't play with Jimmy and Timmy anymore. Eventually, the problem was obviated when Timmy's parents split up, and he, his brother, and his mom moved up to northern Michigan to live with her parents on the family farm.

I'm sure there were some other differences between my family and Timmy's. Our water-sharing arrangement hadn't lasted very long before my folks decided to have a well dug in our own back yard-- a very deep well as it turned out. I guess the well digger went deep looking for some *really good water*—he never found it. Alternatively, I suppose the depth might explain why our water was so hard. All the heavy iron and minerals must have sunk way down to the bottom.

The ringing "Whack!...Whack!...Whack!" of the driver as it hit the well point was quite a novelty for me. But it was the new well pump that attracted the most enduring attention. It was in what we called the "well pit," with the pump on a concrete pad, that was covered with its own little house. My dad built the well house out of concrete blocks, about four feet high, with a flat top covered with roll roofing. I used to pull myself up and stand on top of it all the time. My dad, on the other hand, used to spend a lot of time inside it, trying to get the pump to work. Maybe it only *seemed* that this was always in the middle of the night or the middle of winter.

I'll build a stairway to heaven
I'll climb to the highest star.
Neil Sedaka

CHAPTER TWO

My Space

The bedroom I shared with my big sister, Lynne, was about six feet by ten feet, just big enough for bunk beds and a chiffarobe at one end. There was no room whatsoever for legitimate play, but we still managed to have fun. Sometimes we would make believe we were on a boat or train. More often, we'd just get squirrely and bounce on our knees up and down on the bed. A couple of times, we worked the slats loose and caused the top mattress to fall down onto the lower one. One of the times this happened, I was on the bottom bunk when my sister made the top mattress fall, but it wasn't a disaster. Only one end came down, making my space more interesting and more fun for both of us. Of course my father wasn't very amused when he got home from work and had to put the mattress back into place again. That was the last time we made the mattress fall.

When my little sister, Sandy, came along, a bassinette was added to our tiny room, but as my baby sister outgrew it, it became obvious that what was barely adequate for two wasn't going to work for three. I got to move into the utility room, and at last I had a room of my own. The washing machine and the furnace were in there, too, but the furnace fan going on and off in the night was actually comforting, covering up the spooky, creaky sounds of the night Going from sharing tight quarters with my older sister to, albeit, tight quarters of my own was a little scary and, I guess a little lonely too. My dad left very early in the morning, and I remember slipping into bed with my mother after he'd left. There was a definite and

9

strong feeling that went with these excursions, before she discouraged me from them. It was a feeling of overwhelming comfort and satisfaction, but mixed oddly with a sense of guilt. Oh those Oedipal hormones!

The most dramatic incident during my sojourn in the utility room was the fate of my dragonfly collection. The road past one side of my house turned ninety degrees, just past the house behind us, to create another street. It also went straight a little ways to the edge of the woods, but it wasn't used and was partially overgrown, creating a little meadow. This was a nursery for wild pink, intoxicatingly sweet-smelling roses. It also was a haven for dragonflies and butterflies. The interesting thing about dragonflies to me was the number and arrangement of spots on their wings. I decided one day that I was going to make a dragonfly collection that included all the different spot patterns. I caught six or eight with different spots and pinned them to a piece of cardboard that I put under my bed. I woke up the next morning to a swarm of ants on the floor, feasting on my dragonflies. It was actually fortunate that our ants were "meat" eaters; we never had a problem with carpenter ants.

About this time, instead, a carpenter friend of my parents began an addition to our house. The arrangement was that my father would help, as well as paint his friend's house. The labor, then, was "free," and materials were bought as they could be afforded. When the addition was done, doubling the size of the house, it was all paid for. I got my own real bedroom, my parents got a full-size room, and my sisters got one to share. The rooms actually had honest-to-goodness closets (the lack of closet space in older houses clearly says that people didn't used to have many clothes!). We also added a garage, an enormous asset, given Michigan winters.

***

The urge to have or create a space of our own may well be universal, or perhaps we pick it up from our parents. At any rate, Lynne and I were forever building "forts," behind the couch, with the cushions from the couch, or with chairs and blankets. Outside, we would construct little towns with sticks, stones, leaves, and dirt. When it rained, we would develop elaborate systems of rivers and lakes on the dirt roads in front of or beside the house. Down at our beach, we'd collect Popsicle sticks and use them in the sand to make complex creations.

I don't know exactly at what age Lynne began to eschew this sort of thing. It probably was about the same time she stopped running after and tackling me, whereupon she would pummel my back with her fists. I don't remember what my offense was to deserve such an ignominious response, but that sort of little brother abuse didn't last long before my growing ability to fight back became a deterrent. Throughout the rest of our childhood, Lynne and I had a most cordial relationship. She grew up pretty, popular, and smart, all things I aspired to. I benefitted from being known as her little brother, and she was comfortable with that.

I do know that she didn't participate in the grand underground fort that I and a few of my friends dug in the field a few blocks away from my house. The soil in that particular field was reddish sand that dug easily and smelled good, almost as if it were laced with sassafras roots. We made a series of short tunnels, and anyone watching us surely could have concluded that we had evolved from gophers or moles.

My mother got to see what we were doing each day during construction, because I brought a lot of my work home with me on my clothes and in my pockets. I am sure that she learned early on to *always* check my pockets before washing my clothes, for sand or acorns or whatever. I'll bet she did it cautiously, however, at least after the time I brought home a literal bucket of snakes. It was a surprise, and she screamed a bit, but at least it wasn't concealed. Imagine putting your hand in your kid's pants pocket and pulling out a snake. But it would never have happened; I had more sense than that. Heck, the darn thing might have bitten me.

I feel sorry for any kid who doesn't get an early and hands-on education in dirt. It's now scientifically proven that kids who are allowed to play in the good earth develop a resistance or tolerance to a whole range of otherwise harmful bacteria and are thus a lot more healthy. I got my degree in dirt with honors. You know how honored graduates get those gold cords to wear on their shoulder at graduation? I wore my badge of honor every day in shirt-sleeve weather in the blackened arms of my white tee shirts, where I would wipe my sweaty face.

I *loved* getting dirty; maybe that was the difference between me and both my sisters. My little sister, Sandy, being five years younger than my big sister and three years younger than I, was on her own to dig and build. My friends and I certainly weren't going to let any *little sister* participate in our projects, and Lynne had already gone way beyond the dirt stage.

Sandy was a lot more like me in some ways than I would ever have admitted at the time. We both had problems with our eyes turning in and wore glasses from an early age. We both suffered the teasing of our peers for being "cross-eyed" and "four eyes." A typical middle child, I'm sure I resented my little sister's reflecting my own shortcomings and, especially, any sympathy she got for them, which should have all gone to me. My big sister picked on me a bit, and I passed it on down the line. Mostly, however, I tolerated Sandy when I couldn't ignore her, and ignored her when I could. This went on until I figured out that she was often not only the sole card player available to me much of the time, but a good one at that.

***

Taking up residence in the trees was the next step in my spatial evolution. My buddies and I were frequently planning, building, or occupying a tree fort. These usually were not far off the ground and took advantage of horizontal branches to support some sort of floor. Our most elaborate structure utilized a tree uprooted by an ice storm. One of its large branches was sticking diagonally up into the air. This became the "beam" against which we built a two-story structure, six or seven feet square, from used 2 x 4's and clapboard siding we got somewhere. There was a ladder up into the second level and a hatch out onto the roof. We made small fires on the ground floor and frequently would have to scramble up the hatch onto the roof to escape from the smoke.

My highest tree house, and my most personal space, was the result of an argument with my good friend, Jim, with whom I had regular arguments and fights. Jim moved into the house across the street on one side when I was about eight. He was especially fascinating because not only was he left handed, he had a broken arm. Two years older than I and having moved to Michigan from Arizona, he was a man of the world. He knew a lot of things I didn't and made me aware of this frequently. We were pals, nevertheless, especially during the summer.

The summer I was a rising fifth grader, we had started a low-level tree house in the little woods across from his house and had a disagreement over the design. I was tired of his being a know-it-all, and especially that he usually did know more than I did. I decided I'd make *my own* tree house, and it would be *better* than his. "Better" in this case is a relative term. It was, for sure, higher.

Whatever else I lacked in ability as a child, I *was* the champion tree climber. This seems to have come from an inherent love of high places, although it hasn't developed into anything similar in later life. When I was two, however, my parents told me, I hailed them from the top of the house across the street one day. The neighbor had been working on his roof and left the ladder up. Another time, not that many years later, they told me I shouted down from way up in one of the big trees at the edge of our property, "Hey Mom and Dad look at me!"

It was that very tree where I built my high-rise tree house. Actually it

12

was just a plywood platform, nailed to a crotch of branches fifty or sixty feet up. Getting the materials *up* to the building site required a bit of engineering. Without Jim (who later became a high school shop teacher), I was truly on my own. I had a piece of rope that was maybe twenty feet long. I made a hole in one corner of the plywood and tied the rope to it and started up the tree with the rope. I climbed to the length of the rope, pulled up the plywood, and tied it off. Then I'd climb with the loose end of the rope, tie it off, and climb down and untie the plywood. I repeated the process until I had the plywood in place. The plywood was heavy and bulky, and pulling it through the branches without it's pulling *me* out of the tree was actually quite a feat.

My tree "house" admittedly wasn't much, but it was my refuge, a place I could go and lie on my back, look up into the leaves, and think. I remember well coming home from the first few days of school that year and "running" up the tree to lie on my high-rise deck and rue the end of summer. I don't know if all kids ever have a place like this, but they definitely need one. I think kids have a hard time being deliberately alone these days and alone with their thoughts.

My platform was about halfway up the best climbing tree I ever knew. For one thing, it was one of, if not *the* tallest, trees in the area. From way up in the top, I could see for miles and miles, even if it was mostly the tops of other trees. Another exemplary thing about this tree was that it had a bunch of smaller trunks growing up around it. It was easy to shinny up one of these to catch onto one of the lower branches of the main trunk. From there, the tree had lots of branches, and it was a virtual stairway to heaven. At the top, the trunk split into vertical branches that got smaller and smaller around. I would go up to the top and sway with the wind, holding on to one of these and looking out over the neighborhood. It was a little scary and definitely exhilarating. It also was just about a miracle I was never killed.

But, is it even close to a miracle that so few kids are killed doing what kids like to do? Or, is it merely the normal, natural course of things of a truly human development? Sure, I stepped on something down at the lake one time, wading in a spot where I shouldn't have been, slashed my foot and had to go get it sewn up, but I learned a lesson. Or, rather, I had one reinforced (sometimes kids are slow learners). I already knew not to walk in water unless I was pretty sure there was nothing on the bottom. Here, especially, it was one of the few spots in the lake with a muddy bottom, and walking in mud usually meant pulling off bloodsuckers. So, I was taking a calculated risk, but my benefit and risk calculation was way off. The payoff was only a bobber that someone had lost to a snag.

And, of course, I did get a gash in my forehead in that rock fight with the kid who lived behind me, but I didn't need my mother or father to tell me not to get in any more rock fights—even if I figured I had the advantage. It was easy to see how close I had come to that often-voiced, dire threat of having my eye put out. It wouldn't have been any better, either, if I had put out the other kid's eye.

Yes, I did also get a fish hook in my hand so badly that I couldn't pull it back through because of the barb. Back to the doctor I went, where I learned it was necessary to push the hook through and snip off the barb with wire cutters. It wasn't much fun, so I also learned to exercise more care in whipping my fishing line around.

And, I have to include the time I nearly cut my thumb off with my dad's pocket knife (always whittle *away* from yourself and only in thin strips). Almost cutting my *tongue* off falling off the kitchen table with a bottle cap in my mouth was a little different, since I was so young. I don't actually remember it, so I probably didn't learn anything. The bottle cap was the coated-cardboard kind that used to come on the bottles of non-homogenized milk, and I was probably sucking on the cream that always stuck to the inside. My *mom* learned from this one, not to let us kids put those bottle caps in our mouths…or stand on tables.

Our milk, for many years, was delivered by an honest-to-goodness Twin Pines milkman. In the summer, he would give us kids little chunks of ice to suck on off the block in his delivery truck, and who knows what might have been in that ice? Or in the icicles we'd knock off the roof and suck on in the winter? It's a good thing I never learned a lesson from those things; everyone always said you could get polio from sucking on an icicle from your roof. DDT poisoning was more likely.

Maybe my parents should have kept a little tighter rein on me. After all, as late as 2002, if an American died, there was a one in 35,476 chance it was from contact with sharp objects (assaults not included). There was a one in 2,811 chance it was from drowning. Maybe they shouldn't have let me walk everywhere the way I did. There was a one in 612 chance of dying while walking! It's enough to make you stay home and stay in bed. But one in 4,745 people died that year from falls involving beds, chairs or furniture. Somehow I survived. Somehow almost all of us survived. I believe it was largely through luck, but chance was turned in our favor by our learning to be increasingly careful and responsible for ourselves and our actions.

Home schoolers are not far wrong in thinking that most learning takes place at home or close to home, and not necessarily from books. The scope of my own learning grew as I did, as well as the range of my "school." I would constantly be pushing the envelope, exploring, going farther and farther afield ('awoods', too!). I got lost a few times when I was little, but only ever once in the same place.

What a day for a daydream
Custom made for a daydreamin' boy

Lovin Spoonful

CHAPTER THREE

The Daily Show

There came a time, before too long, when I might set out in the morning
or after lunch and be gone for half a day. I couldn't be gone much longer;
I had *to eat*. (It was too early to go to McDonalds—by about five years,
and then only if I had had a ride to Pontiac, fifteen miles away.) I'd try
to comply with my mother's instructions to tell her where I was going or
what I intended to do.

"Okay," she'd always say. "Be careful, and don't forget to tell me if you
go somewhere else."

"Sure thing, Ma."

There were so many things to do. How did I know what I'd end up
doing, when, and where? The real distance between two points was almost
never a straight line. If there had been cell phones then, I'd have needed
to be in touch almost constantly for my mom to know where I was. All I
know is that I would head out and often be gone for hours, and my mom
would have little idea of where I was or what I was doing. It wasn't that
she didn't care, and I know she worried. But she knew she and my dad
had taught us kids to have good sense and be reasonably careful. She let
us go out into the real world and be real kids. Heaven knows there were
real dangers out there, but how are kids ever to know and appreciate

17

their environment if they aren't allowed to freely play in it, explore it, and experiment with it?

In the morning, I might head for the beach to see what was going on and end up, instead, playing trucks in the sand "plain," under the six-foot sand cliff that one kid was lucky enough to have in his side yard (the glaciers had mixed the soil around so that it varied from sand to clay on different streets.) On the other hand, I might go straight to the lake only to end up a half mile down the shore looking for clams or crayfish and walk back through the woods. I might decide to go froggin' and off to one of several swamps. I'd get a stout stick, creep around the edges, and try to whack a frog before it jumped. For this, I am mortally sorry, especially with the recent rapid demise of the frog population in this country. There was no purpose to it, or at least no good purpose. We mighty frog hunters did skin a few frog legs, but we never ate any; they were much too skimpy. It just goes to show that even kids brought up around nature need to *learn* respect for ecology.

If I started for the woods of a morning, there was no telling what I'd find. In the spring it might be one of those ponds that would form in the low spots from snow melt. These were like magnets and would guarantee wet feet before I got home. On the winter weekends, we'd take our sleds to a part of the woods where there was a string of mossy ponds with steep sides that made treacherous and, therefore, delightful sledding hills. In the summer, those ponds were one of the many great places around to look for turtles and frogs.

Once, some buddies and I found one of the little springs coming up from the ground and feeding those ponds. We felt as if we had discovered the headwaters of the Amazon! We cleared away leaves for 30 or 40 feet to create a flow, and we named it Wolf Creek. How many people get to name a body of water they've discovered? We lay down on the leaves and got a cold refreshing drink of spring water. (Gad, if I'd only had some bottles, I might have started something!) Drinking from a spring was okay; we'd learned that from movies and from TV. It was a good thing we also had learned from TV, albeit erroneously, that people were regularly getting sucked into quicksand, never to return. It surely made us more careful when we were exploring around those ponds.

On a summer's day, I likely might just walk across the street to Jim's. After a few rounds of "Whaddya want to do today"-- "I don't know, what do *you* want to do?" we might decide to go fishing. Then, we might need to go into the woods to find an appropriate sapling to use for a pole. Then, we might have to get on our bikes and ride up to the hardware store to get some black fishing line or some hooks. After a stop at the "leaf pile," (where my family dumped the tons of leaves from raking our yard) to get some worms, there might actually be time to go down to the lake.

We'd mostly fish off a boat dock in the canal along beach property. We'd rarely have trouble catching a bunch, mostly bluegills and sunfish, with an occasional perch or catfish. We'd also rarely catch anything, except maybe a catfish, that was longer than about six inches. A "keeper" would be a five-incher (Jim had a "de-liar," to measure) and if we caught enough, we'd take them home; otherwise, we'd let them go for another day. At home, we'd clean what we'd caught, and in the freezer they'd go. Once or twice a year, our two families would have a fish fry and cook our accumulation on foil with holes poked in it, over charcoal. Then we'd have a good old time trying to separate out the couple of bites of fish from the zillions of bones. There's nothing quite as flavorful as little pan fish caught in a freshwater lake and cooked over charcoal-- *I mean to tell ya* (as my uncle John used to say).

***

At some point, I discovered the public branch library that was all the way across Westacres, the neighborhood on the other side of the woods. Even though it was a couple of miles away, I'd usually walk. I regularly checked out four books at a time (the limit) and it was a bit hard to transport these on my bike (at this stage of my life, baskets on bikes were not cool). The library at my Catholic school was quite limited, so the public library with its relatively copious stacks was a goldmine. Nevertheless, it didn't take that long before I had read my way through all of the dog stories and science fiction books in the children's section and had to beg for special permission to check out books from the adult section.

I have a terrible head for the names of books or movies, but I do remember in particular *Lassie Come Home, Lad, A Dog,* and *Call of the Wild,* classics all. There were a bunch of more contemporary, shiny color-cover, less-than-classic types, but their names escape me. In science fiction, I remember, in particular, *The Haploids, Space Hawk,* and one about all the machinery on Earth freezing up. I forget specific titles for the others, but I read all of the Robert Heinlein books at the time. My favorites were *Door Into Summer, Tunnel in the Sky, Farnham's Freehold,* and *Have Space Suit, Will Travel.* I have had the great pleasure of including *Spacesuit* on my eighth grade reading list and "teaching" it with great enthusiasm.

Despite my predilection for science fiction, and especially space travel,

I was literally down to earth in my reading posture. My position of choice was lying on my side with my head supported in the palm of one hand. This might be on the living room floor or in the front yard. The one drawback was that it caused my hand to fall asleep and my wrist to ache, so it necessitated regular switching of sides. Despite changing, this support system could only be maintained for so long before arms and hands said they had had enough. That length of time would vary in reverse proportion to how entrancing the book was. If a book was *really* good, it might necessitate reading undercover, literally under the covers, with a flashlight when I was supposed to be asleep.

Reading was the perfect compliment to all my real world activities. If my immediate environment gave me knowledge and appreciation for the detail and order of nature, reading let me know the human imagination could create other worlds that could be poignant, frightening, joyous, thought provoking--in a word, fascinating. It also gave me a sense that, while I was somewhat of an expert within the limits of my own little world, the bigger world out there had no limits. There were so many possibilities, so much to know and to do. It is my sense that this knowledge is a form of *intimidation,* today, thrown at kids as a challenge and a huge chore they need to take on. To me, it simply said that life "out there," just like the life with which I was so familiar, was an endless source of new experiences to enjoy.

***

We are, to a large extent, children of our times and our environment. As children, our environment plays a huge role in creating, especially, our sense of life. If the books in my youthful environment gave me a sense of the endless possibilities of life, picking wild berries and other edible treats convinced me of the beneficence of nature. The set of lessons I learned from this was fairly complicated, but the abundance of wild blackberries, black raspberries, strawberries, grapes, nuts, and mushrooms definitely struck me as a good thing.

My dad started me off taking advantage of this abundance, a heritage he got from his father and who knows how much farther back than that. Since my dad soon got too busy to do it himself, the role of family gatherer fell almost exclusively to me. It started in the spring with morel mushrooms. These were such a delicacy to the adults that there was competition for them, at least among several of the other people who had moved up from the same area of Ohio as my parents, including my Uncle John and Uncle Ernie. Hunting these particular mushrooms requires a good deal of skill and possibly some specialized knowledge. According to Uncle John's father, for instance, the craters or pocks in the cap of the morel were ears. If you weren't quiet, any mushroom ahead would hear you coming and pull itself back into the ground. Since it's impossible to move soundlessly through last year's leaves on the forest floor, maybe this explains why I didn't find all that many mushrooms.

My father passed on to me some considerably more useful information and skills, as well as some great character lessons. Morels are painfully difficult to see, especially in the woodsy setting, where they mostly grow. They range in color from black to brown to ivory and easily hide in the leaves on the ground. To find them, you need to walk very slowly and be very observant. My dad used to find one and have me come up to observe it in its natural state, and I'd have a devil of a time seeing it, even when he'd point it out. This slow walking and observation (I'm talking a step or two then scanning the ground for thirty seconds) might go on for some time before I found a single mushroom to confirm that they were even out yet! So the virtue of patience was an absolute necessity.

Perseverance was a must, especially in the hunting grounds around us. I once saw a film on a TV program called *Michigan Outdoors*, in which people were gathering morels by the grocery bag full. In our woods, if we got a lunch bag full it was a successful year. I have often wondered why I was so fascinated and dogged at looking for morels. I didn't like them and didn't eat them then, although I did develop a love for them as an adult. I suppose it was partially the challenge and the competition of finding them. It also had to be that my parents considered them to be a real treat, and finding some was a way I could contribute to the family. This "usefulness" factor, I am sure, played a huge role in my gathering them and other wild things.

Feeling useful certainly doesn't seem to be an inherent need of children, who often go to great lengths to avoid work around the house. It was the same way with me. Chores were definitely a chore. Foraging for edible wild things, and especially berries, was different. Anyone can rake leaves, take out the trash, or wash dishes. In addition to being useful, the produce of nature's supermarket was something I personally liked, out of hand or in the pies, cobblers, jams, and cookies my mother made. I guess that I internalized their value to the rest of my family as well.

There was also the factor of being in on a wonderful secret—all I had to do was pluck the things off the bush or the ground. Wow! When the berries in any given patch were getting ripe, I'd hope against hope

21

that I'd get to them before someone else picked them all, but I rarely had any competition. Apparently no one, much less the other kids in the neighborhood, thought that a bowl of blackberries, sugar, and milk was worth getting hot and sweaty and brutally scratched up. And, as far as I ever knew, only the squirrels thought hickory nuts and black walnuts were worth the effort to free them from their Fort Knox-like shells.

Hot, sweaty, and scratched up was pretty close to how I would get on a regular play day, anyway, and the payoff with berries was special. Specialness came in large part from the supply side. The actual rarity, as with mushrooms, and the difficulty of "production," as with wild strawberries made the gathering special for me. Strawberries grew in the old apple orchard on the other side of one part of the woods. They were tiny and grew close to the ground. It was necessary to pick a bazillion to amount to anything, and do it on hands and knees, which left both boldly stained red. I could imagine Indian maidens once using crushed strawberries to color their lips! The smallness of the berries was compensated for by a proportional concentration of flavor. You haven't tasted a strawberry until you've tasted a wild strawberry. They're far better than even the cultivated ones *used to be*. Most years, there were so many I could spend literally as much time as I had picking them. An excruciatingly sore back, as well as knees, provided the limitation.

Black raspberries were an interesting case. They weren't particularly good as pies or with milk and sugar. They made fantastic jam, however, better than the blackberries to my taste. Since they were the first to get ripe, I always paid special attention to them, and we always had black raspberry jam. I used to love coming across a bush with big, ripe berries still sparkling with morning dew.

Wild grapes were abundant, but their quality varied considerably. It was hard to imagine they'd be good for anything, since most were too sour to eat out of hand and were mostly seeds. Once my mom had made a batch of wild grape jelly, however, I was sold on their value. Hickory nuts were… well, a hard nut to crack. They were easy enough to gather, though, and they were the perfect addition to cookies or in my mom's amazing homemade caramel. Black walnuts were nearly as hard, but made the perfect addition to fudge. Much later in life I finally discovered the best way to crack both, using a large vice to squeeze them till they popped!

I have often wondered what my mom thought of a son who spent more time gathering wild things in the summer than I probably did on all my homework the rest of the year. She would accept my provisions, sometimes matter-of-factly, but usually appreciatively, even though they always meant more work for her. Having grown up "in town," with no tradition of gathering wild things, she didn't have quite the enthusiasm I had. It was okay, however, because I had enough enthusiasm for both of us. I was tapping into the hunter/gatherer heritage of my ancestors. The wild things I brought home were much like the "bacon" my dad brought home. In that, being the provider was a heady experience for me.

I got too busy to pay much attention to wild things when I went to college. For one thing, I got married during my sophomore year and had two children by the time I graduated in five years. A year or so later, I ran across a copy of Euell Gibbons's *Stalking the Good Life*, and I realized how philosophically committed I was to foraging for wild food. I eventually managed to get back to the old neighborhood on a berry-picking expedition. The first time, I found a patch in a whole different area than I had ever picked before, and harvested twenty-five quarts over a few evenings, after work.

When I went back the next year, there were the basements of two soon-to-be houses occupying the berry patch. This was a recurring pattern throughout my childhood, so I did a little exploring, the way I'd always done. It didn't take long until I found an even better patch, spread out conveniently in a field, instead of in a matted tangle on the edge of a woods like the previous one. With this one, someone could have put up a "Pick Your Own" sign and charged the going rate. Over a few days after work and with the help of my wife and kids on a Saturday, we picked forty quarts of high-quality wild blackberries (was I keeping track?—well, *yes*). I will never forget how we'd put my son, who was not yet walking, to sit by a bush so heavy with berries it drooped to the ground. There he would sit, quite contented, picking berries and stuffing them into his mouth.

We moved away after that, and I didn't get back to that neighborhood for years and years. I would guess that, unless someone has planted some nursery bushes in their back yard, the blackberries there are entirely gone. What about the family tradition? My younger sister, one year, lived in a rented house near Niles, MI. At the end of her street, along the St. Joseph River, she found a plethora of black raspberries. She made jam for the family that year. Quite a while later, the year my younger daughter got married, she and her husband-to-be stayed for a few weeks with his parents in Eugene, Oregon. Marionberries (a cross between two cultivated varieties of blackberries) grow along the road like weeds out there, and that's what they are considered to be by local residents. My daughter recognized them as a resource, however, and persuaded her fiancé to pick some with her. *They* made jam for the families that year.

Thanks, Adrienne and Kevin. That jam was better than you'll ever know.

The continuation of the wild berry saga goes on. When my wife and I moved into our present home in a rural, but fast-developing area of North Carolina, I quickly began scouting for wild berries. I discovered blackberry bushes (among the ubiquitous poison ivy!) between the schoolyard and the woods across the road. There aren't a lot of berries, and the quality varies from year to year, but every year I pick enough to make a few pies and a batch or two of jam. Several years ago, I had pretty good year, and Julie and I made enough jam to spread cheer, a half-pint at a time, across my family. The jam turned out great, and my then two and a half year-old grandson, Rowan, declared that this "grampa jelly" was his favorite. The child has good taste, and therein lies the seeds of a continuation of my own grampa's legacy.

Last summer, while visiting Adrienne and Kevin in Western Michigan, Rowan begged me to take him blackberry picking. So, Julie, Rowan, his little brother Shay, and I explored the neighborhood bordering Lake Michigan and found a fine patch of dewberries, a close-to-the ground variety of blackberries. Rowan and Shay excitedly announced each time they picked a berry how big *this* one was, and it was music to my ears. We picked more than enough to renew their supply of grampa jam and the spirits of at least a couple of grampas before me.

Let it snow, let it snow, let it snow

Vaughn Monroe

Chapter Four

Winter Wonderland

Michigan's motto as the "Water Winter Wonderland" is no accident. It's intended to be a commercial lure, to plant the idea in people outside Michigan that the state is a year-round playground. The "wonderland" part of the state motto had to have winter deep in the consciousness of the slogan writers, even if the motto originally was only "Water Wonderland." It was only a matter of time that "Winter," effervescing from every Michigander's pores, would be added. For the kids in my neighborhood, there was no need to belabor the obvious. All we had to do was go outside and the conditions were ideal for some sort of play, and winter, far from being the exception, proved the rule.

The first condition, of course, was the cold. Cold weather for kids was an elixir, one quadrant of the ever-turning wheel of the seasons that was rich with new things to do. Since we did everything with complete involvement and to the point of physical and interest exhaustion, each season's activities were used up by its end, and it was time for the pleasures of the next. Cold gave rise to snow, and snow meant fun.

We kids would wait anxiously for the first snow to fall, because it transformed our world into a wonderland that, unlike Alice's or the others in books, we could physically participate in and enjoy. Early snows changed the brown and gray of late autumn into brilliant white, and since early snow was often wet snow, just as often it stuck to the trees and made not just the ground, but our whole world into a fairyland. The first ritual of the season was to make a snowperson (sometimes a snowman and sometimes a snowwoman) as soon as possible. This meant that our first of the season was often speckled black and white as our rolling snowballs picked up grass and sticks along with the thin layer of snow.

If the snow was deep enough, giving sway to our predilection for kidspace, we'd roll balls into building blocks and make snow forts. These were the precursor to two things, the inevitable snowball fights (wars if they were carried on from snow forts) and the aforementioned exhaustion. Rosy cheeks and cold, wet hands would be juxtaposed with sweaty bodies beneath winter coats, which would often come off, leading to wet clothes from head to foot and a return of the chill. All of this made for time for a break and a retreat to inside comforts. If it was also lunch time, tomato soup and open-faced grilled cheese sandwiches were the ultimate comfort food.

Our oil-burning space heater was great for huddling around and holding frigid red hands over, after coming in from playing outside. It was useful, too, for fixing the cause of those chilly hands. Our gloves would be snow soaked almost the moment we went outside. Leaving wet gloves around or on the stove and being careful not to burn them, would dry them in about the time it would take for our energy to be recharged enough to go back outside.

As soon as the snow accumulated, we also would launch our sleds on anything with an angle of more than five degrees. The steeper the better, of course, and best if we could build a jump in the middle to rattle our teeth. Because woods covered most of the area that wasn't built on, and there weren't very many hills, neighborhood roads were frequently the best surfaces for sledding or saucering on. These usually got better as the season wore on, since they weren't generally plowed, and the snow packed down to a very slick surface. This made driving a car much like driving a bobsled, but that wasn't a concern for us.

As we explored our winter world more widely and thoroughly as we got older, we discovered our favorite sledding hill. It was well back in the woods, and was actually the sloping side of one of the chain three shallow ponds. Our preferred spot was a quite steep, but not very long run. The quick rush and treachery of avoiding small trees made it great kid fun, which we augmented by building a bone-jarring jump on the way down. Aside from having to locate a good spot for sledding was the preparation. The snow had to be packed down or our sled runners would sink in and the sled bottom out. This meant tramping down and up the hill in snow that was deep enough to be usable, and picking out leaves and sticks that would rise to the surface. By the time the hill was ready, we'd be almost too tired to use it. After we had made a bunch of runs and slogged back through the woods home, we'd be burnt out and used up.

The snow-packed roads in the neighborhood didn't keep our school bus from driving back into it to pick us up. Our bus stop was a couple of blocks from our house and, fortunately, out of sight. This combination created ideal conditions for another favorite winter activity. When the school bus let us off on winter afternoons, I and a few other stupid…I mean brave boys would quickly get behind the bus, hunker down, and hold on to the bus's back bumper for a nice little slide on our shoes. We were lucky enough that Mr. Flynn, the bus driver, who from our perspective really didn't like kids, never caught us. We were also lucky enough that none of us ever got hurt.

***

As for the "water" part of our wonderland, the lake and assorted ponds froze early, stayed frozen late, and furnished a host of ways to court frostbite. One thing that probably comes to mind when someone is talking frozen winter water is ice fishing. This never caught on big with me and my immediate friends, despite our devotion to open-water fishing. Unless a guy had an ice shanty, which none of us did, ice fishing meant chopping a small hole in the ice and sitting in one spot, the same way I might have sat fishing in a boat or on a dock or spot on the shore. The thing was, I wouldn't stay in *those* places without moving for more than a couple of minutes if nothing was biting. And that was without freezing my butt off.

I've heard that fish shanties have evolved, about like the cabs on those interstate 18-wheeler trucks. A person very interested in ice fishing these days, or even in just getting away from the house, could spend a day in one watching TV, listening to music, and keeping toasty warm. Not when I was a kid. A shanty was a box, bigger, but still akin in significant ways to an upright freezer. Inside, the plan-ahead ice fisher could have a little kerosene heater to warm his or her hands over, but as far as I could ever tell, anybody who spent much time in one could count on chillin'—in a whole different way than today.

The purpose of the shanty was mostly to break the wind. It also provided a dark interior, which allowed the serious fisher to see down into the sizeable hole chopped in the ice, in order to spear any large fish that came into view. This large hole was the undoing of my father's ice fishing aspirations. His first winter in Michigan, he built an ice shanty, hauled it out onto frozen Middle Straits Lake, and dutifully chopped his hole. Unfortunately, before the thing was fairly broken in, it was broken into. Some pranksters disassembled it and stuffed the pieces into the hole in the ice.

One of the more sophisticated of the contraptions that I and my various friends concocted was an ice boat to ply the winter lake at exhilarating speeds. I think my pal Jim and I got the idea from an old *Mechanics Illustrated* issue. There was a pile of these around from somewhere (I know my dad didn't subscribe), and they were full of great ideas. Using these "scrap" magazines was a perfect way to start our project. Jim and I used the blades off some old ice skates for the runners, left over 2 x 4's for the frame, and a rake handle (I think) for the mast. For the sail, we cut a piece out of one of my dad's well-used paint drop cloths. The advantage of this was that our sail was not only real canvas, it was already decorated in a multi-colored abstract of paint blotches. Our functional design had three nailed-on runners, one on the point of our narrow triangular body and the other two on the ends of a perpendicular bar across the base of the triangle. We finished this baby with a paint job of two-tone blue enamel. It was awesome! It was also awfully heavy to haul down to the lake.

Thinking about the methodology for building our iceboat helps me to understand one reason why so many country folks used to have "junk" all over the place. That's what they used to make new stuff, as they needed it. They cobbled together old pieces and parts, and they never knew what they might need, so they saved everything. My parents didn't subscribe to this economic school of thought at all (except for in our garage), and a junky yard to us was simply a junky yard. But I confess to being a country boy to the extent that I always had a "junk drawer," one drawer in my room designated for "stuff I might somehow, someday need. It evolved over the years, as my idea of things it was important to save did, into mostly love letters, a few old photos, and programs from events I'd gone to or been a part of. Housed in a cardboard box, my junk has traveled thousands of miles, moving with me over the years. The last entries into it were more "love letters"—from my daughter, the college year she spent in France-- and various handmade cards from all of my kids when they were small. I guess I need to rename it. You know what they say about one man's junk. This is definitely treasure to me.

How did the ice boat work? Did I mention that with that blue paint it *looked* great? Yeah, and it might have worked great, too, except for the snow. It's a rarity that Michigan lakes are both frozen enough to walk on *and* snow free. The lake that year in particular was never snow free. The snow slowed our blades and our ambitions to zip across the lake at warp speed. We should have known, since the snow had the same effect on skate blades when they were still connected to the skates. Most of the time lake skating was spent pushing a snow shovel to clear off a space to skate, and then being too tired to use it. Ah, but then it was ready for the next time—if it didn't snow.

Why do I keep sighing, not sad, but sighing?
I'm young and free, and suddenly
it's spring.

Frank Sinatra

CHAPTER FIVE

Spring!

The pond was there. The ice, turned a soft, cloudy white, nevertheless glistened with a thin layer of water that continually evaporated and refreshed itself in the bright sunshine. I stepped gingerly onto the ice, sideways with one foot, gradually transferring weight from the foot still on the ground. As the pressure on the ice's edge grew, it either held or it didn't, and I ended up with a wet foot or not. Why did I run this kind of test over and over through the springs of my Michigan childhood? Because the pond was there.

Earlier, as winter was taking over, I had performed similar tests on the pond, on mud puddles, and on the lake, eager to walk on water. I had chopped holes in the ice and seen it thicken as winter did. Now, the thick ice was the carcass of a dead or dying winter, and I needed to kick it to see which it was. There was also the fact that spring ice was really cool to walk on. It wasn't crisp and crackly like winter ice; it was soft and mutable. It would sag with a muted warning, but if I kept moving, it wouldn't break--most of the time. Often enough, wet feet and pant legs raised the question of, "Why?" from my beleaguered mother. I don't remember what my excuses were, but they couldn't have been much more than, "Because it was there."

I suppose I was also testing the *genuineness* of a warm-day harbinger of spring. Sunny days in March brought out other precursors that were as fickle as the weather that produced them. The steadily dripping icicles on the eaves of my house might go back to freezing on their tips, making them even longer. Or, they might be truly giving up their substance and their very grip, soon to be broken crystal crashing to the ground. The overnight, ever-so-faintly-sweet sapcicles, hanging from maple trees branches, signaled vitality coursing back into the trees. The sun could quickly make them into mere wet spots, but a drop in temperature would easily turn them back to ice. I hadn't internalized the fickleness of spring long before I became aware of the apocryphal schedule for March: "In like a lion, out like a lamb." Even as I became aware of it, I also knew its irony, since the actual progression was more often than not just the opposite. As much as I enjoyed winter fun, it had begun to get old by March. An entire season is a very long time for a child (especially if it involved going to school), since it represents a large portion of his or her entire life. I was ready to move on, and warm, sunny days in early March were as enticing as cider and donuts in fall.

***

Most winters, there was a good accumulation of snow on the ground as March marched in. Combine this with unseasonable warmth and sun, and the result was one of my favorite things—water. And it wasn't just water, but flowing water. There was great joy in an early spring melt. I think it was, as much as anything, a vital affirmation of Nature. The wheel of the seasons was turning, and ice was turning back to water, just as it was supposed to. Gravity was pulling the water down into the Earth or causing it to flow inexorably to ponds and lakes, in either case to awaken and sustain new life and new growth. Everywhere there were kid-size rivers and pools as in a good rain, but the sun was shining! Not only that, I could actually *smell* the melting snow--after a winter of smells being lost in the bottom of the deep freeze. And, of course, there was the promise of grand things to come.

By the end of March, as likely as not, the weather was very lion-like. The accumulation of snow was usually gone, but that surely didn't mean that it couldn't snow some more. The official first day of spring, in substance, might well be just another late winter day. Inevitably, though, the days got longer, the sun came out, and there was gloriously perfect warmth over the land. Everything seemed to want to be out in the sun. Maybe it was only supply and demand at work, but there was celebration in again hearing the buzz of a bee or seeing the first robins. Like no other time, garter snakes and an occasional blue racer could be heard rustling the dry leaves as they busied themselves, fresh from their winter nap.

***

By the time spring had officially come around, the sport of the season was marbles. There is some primeval connection with kids between certain activities and seasons. Somehow, the urge to engage in certain activities comes on at the same time of year or with the same weather. In early spring, for us, it was marbles. It didn't matter too much how cold it was. I can remember playing with hands so chilled it was hard to shoot. This was risky, because marbles was a deadly serious transaction. For kids who didn't have a whole lot of *stuff*, and that included not a lot of marbles, each one was valuable. If a kid was fortunate enough to have a few purie or cat's-eye boulders or that greatest treasure, a steely boulder, the risk of losing one made entering into a match for it a sobering proposition, despite the possibility of winning another. Losing from my limited marble collection was akin to losing from my dollar or two stake in family penny-ante poker games. It was just as disappointing, and even more so, since each marble was an identified component of my wealth, unlike the indistinguishable nickels and dimes.

We never played any organized marbles games; everything was freelance and freehand. We'd wander around the playground looking for a match. Each match required negotiations to set the stakes and the rules. The object was to find someone suspected to be not as good a player, who was willing to risk a marble that was better than I was risking. There was interplay between the two, and a perceived equilibrium needed to be reached before a match could happen. The more highly skilled person, although often risking more, generally had the "house edge," and came out ahead in the long run. By the time baseball weather came around, marbles had become passe', and those kids lucky enough to have had a winning season put their marbles away for another day.

***

The melted snow, along with spring rains, created mud, and on our dirt roads, it was serious. When I was a little kid, mud meant having to wear those clunky rubber boots that sucked at my shoes and socks, trying to take them off. Kids from the new subdivisions with paved roads more often wore galoshes that easily fit over their shoes and were also called "rubbers." It always cracked us up, as older kids, when we'd mimic the nuns at Our Lady of Refuge school telling the little ones, "Don't forget to put on your rubbers." As older kids, we of course, were far too sophisticated to wear boots and inevitably ended up with muddy shoes, which made our mothers even less happy than mere wet feet. Otherwise, mud was just blah; it had none of the attraction of dirt or water alone—a kind of negative synergy. When it refroze at night or on colder days, the mud turned into hard ruts and ridges that tripped up walkers, created obstacle courses for bike riders, and sent drivers to the repair shop for wheel alignments or new shock absorbers.

Neither did early warm spells do anything to relieve the grayness of the bare trees or the brown blanket on the still sleeping ground. With the snow gone, everything was, in fact, dreary, and when the cold returned, the scene was frozen in place. Thus began the "winter" of my discontent, the grey skies, the cold rains, the sharp winds that seemed to go on forever. This was the time, if ever, when "Maaaaaaahhhhm, there's nothin' to do," might come closest to being true. Sure, there was the neglected chemistry set or microscope that provided a few hours of relief, and maybe the attic needed exploring again for one afternoon. There were books to read, but after a winter of forced school reading, that had limited appeal. There were card games to play, but how many games of double solitaire or casino or gin rummy could I stand to lose to my little sister? What had been a welcome warming station from playing outside in the snow and a refuge from bitter cold sub-zero days, now was an incubator for cabin fever.

The out-of-doors called insistently, but this was the one time of year when it was unappealing. Despite the chill that was far more penetrating than mid-winter cold, I made brief forays into the woods or down to the lake, hoping like the dove from the Ark to return with a green twig that signaled salvation. Then, when I had just about forgotten what spring was like, the shadbush trees would pop, white and welcome doves from the woods. Overnight, the rush was on to see who could be next: bloodroots, spring beauties, violets, trout lilies, and trilliums put on their best to welcome spring. Then, the mayapples unfolding and the wild geraniums adding their lovely lavender to the mostly yellows and whites, would signal time to look for morel mushrooms. The season was open, the game was on, and it was time to rock and roll!

***

There's a scene in Forrest Carter's *The Education of Little Tree*, both the movie and the book, that I've always found to be as true as it is inspirational. Little Tree, half Caucasian and half Cherokee, follows a small spring-fed branch in an Appalachian woods and finds his "secret place." "It was a little way up the side of a mountain and hemmed in with laurel. It was not very big, a grassy knoll with an old sweet gum tree bending down. When I saw it, I knew it was my secret place, and so I went there a lot." Little Tree was too young to keep a secret, so he tells his Cherokee grandma. She wasn't surprised, which itself surprised Little Tree. His grandma tells him all Cherokee have a secret place, and "she reckined most everybody had a secret place, but she couldn't be certain, as she had never made inquiries about it."

I have never made inquires either, and I can't speak for others. All I know is that the time and place where I grew up was rich in potential for secret places, and I had, in fact, more than a few. Most of them were easily available to anyone with open eyes—like the various wild berry patches--a fact that didn't diminish their specialness, since most people weren't looking. Others begged to be shared with a best friend—like the tiny spring-fed brook I discovered in the woods. Still others were entirely private, which was a goodly part of their value. The tall maple at the edge of my family's property and the edge of the woods, which I could climb to its top, was that place for me. It was a place I returned to over and over, a place where I could literally be alone above the world, a place that lent itself to both deep thought and free-form meditation. It unquestionably facilitated my philosophical bent, which continues to this day.

A large part of the wonder of spring was its hand-lettered invitation to me to revisit familiar secret places or discover new ones. Winter had its own places, but the inside ones were less likely to be secret, and outside ones were less comfortable and inviting to stay. Spring still extends its invitation to me, but it seems now as if the best places are the ones I visit in my memory.

From the locker to the blanket,
From the blanket to the shore,
From the shore to the water,
Guess there isn't any more.

Brian Highland

CHAPTER SIX

The Beach

Oakland County, has nearly 400 named glacial lakes and many more as yet unnamed. It was only natural, in every sense of the word, for kids to want to spend as much time as possible down at the nearest lake. My street led directly to our neighborhood beach on Middle Straits lake, about a quarter of a mile away. It was far enough to make getting to the lake on a hot day a little burdensome, and to enhance the relief of slipping into the cool water. It was also far enough that once I was there, it took a lot (near starvation, for example) to get me to leave. I spent a lot of time at The Beach.

The actual beach was sandy, as was the lake bottom. The water was perfectly clear, and since it was spring fed, it never got so warm that it wasn't refreshing. There was a beach house, run most of the years of my youth by a rather gruff but lovable local widow, who was also one the customers on my newspaper route. Rain or shine, the Beach House was redolent with the smell of suntan lotion and wet swim suits. It had changing rooms and a perpetually wet cement floor, gritty with sand. There were no showers, only an outdoor faucet for washing the sand off of feet. Showers would have seemed peculiar to us kids, since to us the lake water itself was at least as clean as any tap water. In fact, there were some adults who would bring a bar of soap and take a "bath" in the lake, something I always resented as polluting the water.

The Beach House also had a concession area that was a cornucopia of sensory delights for kids. These ranged from penny candy such as Black Jacks, candy dots, and Lik-m-Aid to toasted Stewart sandwiches that *smelled* so delicious. Smell and sight were the senses most often treated by much of the goodies for sale, since most of the time we kids didn't have more than a nickel or a dime at a time.

Given the heat of summer, if a kid had a dime, it would likely be best spent on something cold, and that usually meant Popsicles. My favorite flavor of Popsicle was root beer, followed closely by banana, and if I had the seven cents to buy one, I'd be hoping one of those flavors was in the freezer. The standard flavors, of course, were cherry, lime, orange, and grape. Nominally, it would be more accurate to say red, green, orange, and purple, which was also the color they turned your tongue and your lips. Then, there was that new flavor, that we savvy kids just called "blue Popsicles." I think they were supposed to be raspberry flavored, but as with blue moon ice cream, no promotional effort was made to enhance the image as something natural, that originated on a bush or a tree. They certainly weren't *blue*berry, because then they would have had to be *purple*, and purple was already taken.

Any color was far preferable on a hot day to nothing, and on different days I might be in the mood for any one of them. More likely, if I had a few more cents, I'd go for a fudgesicle, which in those days was bigger, and much more worthy of the name than today's version. Pushups, orange (and occasionally lime or raspberry) sherbet in a tube, were the same price and very good. Going up the scale, an ice cream sandwich was a dime, and a drumstick a whopping twelve cents. I hear they are likely to stop making pennies pretty soon. That says a lot, doesn't it? A penny or two in those days made a big difference. Without pennies it would have been difficult to do pricing for the things we kids liked. And, what about *penny* candy?

My favorite cold treat of all was probably the moderately-priced Creamsicle. Now there was a bargain. Real vanilla ice cream on a stick, with a layer of orange sherbet on the outside. That had to be the greatest combination since Reeses peanut butter cups married chocolate to peanut butter. Of course we could get those frozen, too, as well as a small three-cent candy bar called a Milk Shake. An interesting variation on the Creamsicle was the Dreamsicle. These weren't around long, and I might have even doubted that they were at all, except my wife affirms it (she worked at a beach concession stand across and at the other end of the lake). A Dreamsicle was vanilla ice cream covered with lime sherbet. It must not have been very successful, and in truth, it wasn't nearly as good as its cousin. It was, at least, an interesting variation for a while.

One thing The Beach usually lacked was a lifeguard. I can remember only two years we had a lifeguard, a female college student. She had a regular schedule, but couldn't be there all the hours The Beach was open. She was pretty mild mannered, not bossy, absolutely not full of rules and restrictions. Mostly, she got a good tan and swam out on her paddleboard a couple times a day. I can't help but contrast this with public pools today, with their three or four lifeguards in their towers overseeing the spots where the diving boards *used to* be (taken out for liability sake) and badgering kids about breaking the rules. Interestingly enough, in 2005, in Oakland County, with a population of over 1,200,000 and its hundreds of lakes, there were only eight drownings. Four of them were in swimming pools.

***

When I was a kid, parents and older siblings helped us learn how to swim, but mostly we taught ourselves. I will remember forever running through the shallow water as a two or three year old and lying on the bottom in the shallow water pretending to swim—just as I've watched other little kids, including my grandchildren, do ever since. In between galloping and faux swimming, if I'd stand still in the water, and as if I were the most interesting thing in the world, a formation of the ubiquitous minnows would fly in to investigate. If I was still for a little longer, they'd begin to nibble on my toes. I was, as a matter of principle (boys must try to catch fish) forever trying, with a swipe of my hand, to catch some. A principle of nature, however, is that boys can't catch minnows by hand.

Before too long, I graduated to the Little Raft. This was metal, on legs in about two and a half feet of water, and about three feet wide by about twenty feet long. It was the first challenge and adventure for us little kids. I remember first jumping off into my mother's arms, and after a bit of that, screaming "Mommy, watch me!" as I jumped off into the water. It was such an accomplishment, and I felt so BIG. After mastering the Little Raft, I was on my own, but the rule was: Don't go *past* the Little Raft. Uh huh.

The next major goal was the Big Raft, probably fifteen feet square and in seven or eight feet of water. I don't know how many summers it took, but before I could actually swim, I had figured a way to push the envelope and get to the Big Raft. I would bounce up and down on one foot, pushing my head up out of the water. This, combined with being able to swim *under*water, made me feel comfortable and confident, and ultimately helped me to learn to swim well *on top* of the water. Without the freedom to experiment, I'm sure it would have taken me far longer.

Once I had achieved the Big Raft, there was no stopping me. I could dive off and easily swim underwater back to where I could stand up. Swimming quickly became a matter of course, and I was ready to become a roughhouser-in-training. For young males, normal activity on the Big Raft consisted of diving or jumping off, pulling ourselves back up, and standing, sitting, or lying in the sun, then repeating the cycle. If there were several guys on deck, however, the male gaming instinct would often kick in. This might manifest itself as seeing who could make the biggest cannonball splash or who could dive off and swim the furthest underwater. It could also be who could do the best back flip off the raft, or we would challenge *ourselves* to swim all the way across the lake.

Frequently, however, competition would ascend to the royal entertainment of King of the Castle, that is, who could push whom off the raft. This resulted in some titanic battles, some scratches, slips, bruises, and so on. It was foolish, I suppose, but it was a lot of fun. Did we guys push girls off the raft? Well, we didn't *wrestle* with them. But, provided we didn't think they'd actually get angry, we weren't entirely adverse to giving a little push here and there. Having the girls go off into the water, voluntarily or otherwise, provided the opportunity for a little chivalry in giving them a hand to pull them back up onto the raft. In pulling the girls up, their bathing suit tops would often fall away, revealing the most lovely of views, but of course we boys never looked. We were just trying to help.

If things were slow, a few of us guys might decide to swim over to the High Dive. This was a raft with a ten foot high diving board on it. It was up the shore a little from The Beach, and in deeper water. It went with one of the houses to which people only came out on holidays or weekends. Since it had no 'Keep Off" signs on it, we figured it was okay to use, but just to be safe, we only swam over there on weekdays. I can't recall that we did any roughhousing there. Since we were "guests," we were on our best behavior. Besides, jumping or diving off that high board was thrill enough.

With all our roughhousing, self-taught swimming, and lifeguard deficit, no one was ever seriously hurt at The Beach in the fifteen years I swam there. Nor did anyone drown or come close to it; nor, to my knowledge, did anyone drown in our lake or any other lakes in the immediate area.

I thought about this and some of the other things I've done that involved some degree of calculated risk, when my then 16 year-old son told me he and some buddies were going to jump off an old railroad bridge into the Huron River, when we lived in Ann Arbor. My first reaction was to ask him if he figured it was safe. He told me they knew exactly where and why it was safe to jump and where it wasn't and that other kids had been doing it for years. I told him to be careful, and he said he would. Part of me wished he had asked me to come along.

Among the other simple pleasures that were open to kids, subject only to common sense, were swimming in the rain and swimming at night. Night swimming created a complete reversal, most nights, in the temperature differential between air and water. It was freaky and fun to go into the water to get warm from the cool night air, rather than to get cool from the hot sun. Cold rain had the same effect, and felt like little pin pricks on bare skin if it was coming down hard. It was also very cool to go just under the surface and look up at the rain falling into the water. I always kept my eyes open under water. At night, this would create rainbow halos around the lights on The Beach.

On days when there were no interesting girls at The Beach or guys to roughhouse with, the lake itself was endlessly fascinating. I generally had my mask, snorkel, and fins with me, and was ready to play *Sea Hunt* for hours. Once again, I learned more about the natural history of the lake by actually exploring it than I ever would from a class at school. One of the things I looked for was fish, especially big ones, to try to discover where they hung out and improve my chances of maybe catching one fishing. I was endlessly optimistic that I'd see one of the really big bass or pike or who knows what.

I also would explore the bottom, especially of the swimming area, for treasure. The anticipation was better than the rewards, and usually all I found were some detached band-aids or barrettes. Every once in a while, though, I'd find a coin or someone's lost bracelet. One little "treasure" that occurred in abundance in the area just to one side of The Beach was clams. Though I quickly was disabused of the possibility of finding pearls in one, I did raid the clams here occasionally for fish bait. Pieces of clam were supposed to be good, but you couldn't prove it by my success.

Many days I'd just take the tour up the shoreline sightseeing, as it were. The awareness of being in an entirely different world was awesome. There were no houses on this wooded stretch of shore, and since these excursions were almost always on slow weekdays, there were no boats or anything else to disturb my reverie. I would have to lift my head out of the water every now and then to check on the other world. It was almost scary to be removed from it for too long. (This may have reflected all the science fiction I had read, or maybe watching the *Twilight Zone*.) The ripples in the sand from waves; the narrow green shafts of wild rice; the colorful perch, whose body shape was so different from the predominant bluegills and sunfish: these were my museum, a cross between natural history and fine art.

***

One of the anomalies of growing up where I did was that none of the residents of my neighborhood had a power boat. There were a few across the lake, I think, but most of the power boats on the lake were from the "city people" who came out on weekends. Consequently, I never learned how to water ski very well. I did have friends in high school, who lived on different lakes and had boats, who could slalom like a pro, or even ski barefoot. I, however, could barely stay up on two skis once around the lake. By the same token, none of the kids from my little "swim club" would have been worth a darn as competitive swimmers, without a lot of coaching and training. None of the high schools in the immediate area even had a swim team, or a pool, and the skills I gained from my environment were utilitarian or incidental rather than polished or especially efficient.

We kids were a lot like the houses we lived in. Almost all of them were old fashioned; many of them had formerly been summer cottages. None of them were elegant, but all of them had the advantage of a great location. Some had been added on to or modernized, but all of the modernization was built around a core that reflected the nature of the neighborhood. While I lived there, not that many new houses were built, and only a few on the whole lake. None of them was particularly "modern" and none of them grand. In fact, three-fourths or more of our side of the lake was woods or marsh right up to the water, with no houses at all. Since then, all of the vacant lots in the neighborhood and property on the lake have been built on. The woods is now the home of "estates," with their obligatory palaces. Only wetland preservation laws have saved the marshes. I'm sure that the lake buzzes with power boats now and that many more kids get a chance to become good skiers and join the high school swim team. That's progress, I suppose.

***

The areas on either side of the snack bar in the Beach House had the magical name of "changing rooms." They were used mostly by adults. Adults seemed to have a need to have labels on things and designated areas so they knew what to do, where, and when. The name was accurate,

42

however. When adults went through a changing room, something remarkable happened. They went in with street clothes on, well adapted for a life on land, a life of multiple responsibilities and roles. When they came out, they were (un)dressed for relaxation and fun. We neighborhood kids had no need of the magic of changing rooms. We would wear our bathing suits to the beach and sometimes keep them on all day. We were in and out of the water, wet and dry, home for lunch, off on a bike ride. Life was magic; we were changing constantly.

Bathing suits did facilitate one of life's most dramatic changes, the change from being on the beach to being in the water. There was a whole range of possibilities here. In the spring, it was the difference between relative comfort and half freezing to death. By mid-summer, the change was from sweaty, tongue-hanging languor to cool, exhilarating pleasure. It never was quite that simple, however, at least not if I'd been out of the water for a while, and especially for the first time in of the day. There were different ways, different styles, to approach the transition, and I, and everyone else, would vary according to circumstances. Regardless of circumstance, however, there always is that moment of excruciating but sweet suffering that made what followed that much better.

Some of us, some of the time, would literally take a running leap into the water. The whole-body electric shock of hitting the cool water was explosive, but it changed to relief almost at once as the sensual "ahhhhh" came out as a stream of grateful bubbles. This approach was my preferred one, sometimes with the embellishment of a front flip into the water, if the object wasn't just to get into the water, but to impress someone in doing it.

The complete opposite approach was to spread out the shock by going in gradually. Personally, I think this is the method of the true masochist or the person who will never learn that the anticipation is not only worse than the pain, but that the two together are exponentially worse! Under this method, you either walk out gradually into deeper water, or you lower yourself several inches at a time in increments. Either way, you get to feel the line of demarcation cutting its way up your legs until—mmm hmm, you know. There are two places especially sensitive to the sweet pain of temperature change: where your legs come together and where your belly begins. True gradualists will suffer both as they ease in all the way up to their chins. Yikes! And, they don't get the same payoff in instant relief. A lot of women who didn't want to get their hair wet used to go in this way.

True gradualists were few; in fact, there probably was a normal bell curve, with the gradualists at one end and the running leapers at the other. In between were the majority who would wade out a ways, sometimes going up on tip toes to avoid those sensitive areas as long as possible, and then dive into the water.

***

The Beach was a world unto itself. It was a fascinating, educational, and fun world, with little of the downside of the rest of the world. It was possible to get bored here, but a kid really had to work at it. The Beach was a life poem. Its smell alone was a metaphor for everything a kid might expect. The crucible of sand on the hottest, brightest days radiated a purgatorial scent of roasted skin cells, sweat, and evaporated lake water-- a warning to move on quickly to the water. In the winter, the wind, blew across the ice to pile up frozen waves one upon the other at the lake's edge. Iced with frosty foam, it carried a lack of smell so palpably that it made way for the phantom scent of frozen nostrils, with just a hint of genuine danger.

In between these two extremes, The Beach was wafts of charcoaling burgers, wet bathing suits, bodies broiling in suntan oil, bubble gum, and pop corn. Underlying all this was the spice of dead seaweed mixed with a touch of live fish. All of it translated to the promise of physical pleasure, fun, romance, discovery, and a catalog of possibilities for every kind of dream being fulfilled.

Neville Shute published *On the Beach* in 1957, and the movie version came out in 1959. I was too young to be interested at the time. When I finally read the book, it struck me how the hopeless metaphor of beached humanity, which seemed to stand for the reality of the grown-up world, was so starkly distinct from the optimism of my beach, where even on the coldest winter day or the hottest summer day, relief was nearby and in my power.

When I think back on all the crap I learned in high school,
It's a wonder I can think at all.
But then, my life of education hasn't hurt me none;
I can read the writing on the wall.
Paul Simon

CHAPTER SEVEN

Be True To Your School

I'd like to think that my parents intuitively understood the importance of early environment to education and picked the spot where I grew up as a "good place to raise children." However they understood it, it *was* a good place for kids and a virtual university in the round.

I went to earth science class back to the earth, discovering the relative merits of sand, clay, and the rich black dirt in the woods for creating little towns, building forts, or planting a garden, respectively. In biology, I cleaned fish, watched spiders eating their prey, pulled bloodsuckers off my legs, and peered into birds' nests to look for eggs hatching. Physics was done in field research: adjusting the balance of teeter totters to accommodate kids of different weight, waxing slides by sitting on waxed paper to reduce resistance, and building ramps for bikes, sleds, and toy trucks.

By the time I got to kindergarten at Scotch School, the ubiquitous worksheets were *slow* by comparison. What was matching three balls or even three green things to matching up black and yellow swallowtails with mourning cloaks and knowing that, as butterflies, they were different from moths? And what was matching a coat on a worksheet and a hat, or an umbrella and a raincoat, to matching up found bird feathers to goldfinches, blue jays, and red-headed woodpeckers? I knew that water flowed downhill and that I could determine which spot was lower by cutting a channel between two puddles and seeing which way the water flowed. I knew a good deal about astronomy from scrutinizing and wondering about the dark, starry skies. Research was a continuous, real-world process, often needs-based, but just as often stimulated by, and in turn stimulating, intellectual curiosity.

Fortunately, when I began my graduate studies in kindergarten, my teacher, Miss McGuire, was gentle, kind, and mother like, and I loved her. This was so because I had already conceptualized "mother" as someone who was always there when I needed her; someone who gave hugs and comforted me when I hurt myself; someone who read entertaining stories and nursery rhymes to me; someone who was safe, interesting, resourceful, and loving. Unfortunately, I had to share Miss McGuire with a bunch of other kids.

One thing that was a little beyond my understanding in kindergarten, because I had little experience to which to relate it, was the behavior of some of the children. I had never known kids who were randomly mean. My sisters and I could be mean to one another at times, but that was different; we knew each other and had reasons, however trivial or fleeting, for our feelings and actions. How could a kid I didn't even know walk up and hit me, or take something away that I was playing with, or say something nasty? Another revelation provided by the "socialization" process came from seeing kids bullying or teasing other kids. The choice of physically intervening, tattling, or "minding my own business" taught me the life-shaping lesson that the meek shall inherit the guilt.

On the other end of the interaction spectrum was another almost-new thing, romantic love. All boys, perhaps, have a share of Oedipal love, but that was way different from what I felt for Susie in my kindergarten class. She lived over on the other side of my neighborhood, near Hooper's pond (I would be reminded of her many times in the future when I would go "frogging" there). My older sister was already friends with her sister, so I guess that's how Susie and I got together. I can almost remember what Susie looked like. I can definitely remember going to her house in the afternoon and coloring together, and I can remember the sweet, compelling affection I felt for her. It had the same unmistakable feel as later young love. Even more than being a prototype for love, however, I'm sure it created a yearning in me for it, since what I remember best was suffering early heartbreak when Susie and her family moved away at the end of the school year.

Kindergarten was also different in being very organized and a little bit pushy, belying Ms. McGuire's kind personality. As students, we were always supposed to be doing something specific and doing it in the "correct" way. In my pre-school natural world, everything was integrated and made sense; I had a rudimentary understanding of natural laws. In school, the organization was arbitrary and beyond understanding. The only thing to do was to follow directions, because I was completely out of my element and not in control. So, I sat at the table I was assigned and did the worksheets I was told to do. I played the tambourine or tapped on a block and drank my milk when the assigned times came for each. Then, I got on my assigned bus and went home much wiser, or at least more experienced, in the ways of human society.

First grade carried a much bigger shock. Unlike kindergarten, it was an all-day affair, and I went to Our Lady of Refuge, a Catholic school. My wife started school at the same time in the next community over, under the same circumstances. She swears, and her family backs this up, that the nuns scared her so badly the first day that she left. She started walking home, a distance of about five miles! A neighbor recognized her on the side of the road and gave her a ride home. Her parents enrolled her in the nearby public school, and there she stayed, quite happily.

I stayed in Catholic school, and I learned, straightaway, lessons that were essential to success in school for the next eight years. The knowledge of order I had acquired in kindergarten was elementary, indeed. Now, I learned to sit up straight in my desk, in my straight row of desks. I learned not to talk unless I had permission to talk from an adult. I learned that I was just one face in a crowd of thirty-five kids and that the easy way to get by was to be orderly and, thereby, not be noticed. If I *wanted* to be noticed, I learned there were two ways to accomplish this: be even a little bit bad or be extra good. It seemed to me, however, that either of these extremes was not so much a matter of choice as it was of chance.

I learned that everyone has a role in life that he or she was put here for. That lesson was obvious from the way the nuns treated different children. It was also clear to even a first-grade brain that we all were expected to stick to our roles but still do our best, within our God-given limitations. Our roles depended upon how old we were, how smart we were, how typically well-behaved we were, who our parents were, and what religion we were, effectively in reverse order. One's religion was, of course, the critical factor, *eternally*; the chances of anyone's going to heaven who wasn't a Catholic were slim indeed. But, since *we* were *all* Catholic, we had a good chance. We were expected to live up to (or down to) the rest of our circumstances

How well we *accepted* and *used* those God-given circumstances was the key factor, both moral and practical. The nuns left no doubt that this determined both our day-to-day and our eternal fate.

In first grade I learned that Sister Rosiland was The Boss and that she derived her absolute authority in a line from the principal, the parish priest, the archbishop, the Pope, and ultimately from God. I am sure that parents were not in that line. The Fourth Commandment told us "Honor thy father and thy mother," but that was only *outside* of school. Our parents were okay for *domestic* authority, but for educational or moral matters, we needed to listen to God's handmaidens. For those moral issues, we had our green "catechisms," and we darn well better be able to recite the articles of our "faith" by heart--or else.

Speaking of outside the classroom, at lunchtime, we had a substantial break after we finished our lunches from home. It seems to me that the lunch period was an hour in total, which left at least a half hour for recess. We were allowed to go outside (in fact, I think we *had* to) and roam the substantial church and school grounds. Of course, we couldn't break any Commandments on the playground, and our consciences were our guide. Other than that, we were almost completely unsupervised. I suppose this was to give the nuns time to go back to the convent for lunch, although I don't think any kid less experienced than, say, a sixth grader, could have imagined that nuns did such an earthly thing as eat lunch.

It has intrigued me for many years, and especially as a middle-school teacher, that we kids were just turned loose. I guess it was the educational counterpart to mothers at that time turning their kids loose on a summer morning, often not to see them until lunch or even dinner. There must have been an *expectation* that kids would behave themselves or at least not do anything terribly wrong. I'm fairly certain that kids pretty universally expected much the same thing. I know in my case and with the kids on my playground, you'd better, *by God*, behave yourself. If you didn't, you had Sister Domitilla (I swear), the principal, to deal with, plus your own conscience. The latter would be activated by the good sisters, even if it wasn't functional on its own.

There *was* the threat of punishment, but I believe that kid self-control came even more from our expecting that this was the way good kids acted. If we strayed from that expectation even a little bit, we were doing something bad. I don't think that any kid really wanted to be bad. For me, I know the expectation of what a good kid did and didn't do came in large part from the books I read, from the TV programs I watched, from the movies I saw. I shudder to think about the expectations and the models kids get from the same sources today.

Expectations in school worked in another other way, too. Kids got *tracked* by a lot of factors; character was one of them. Today, teachers and students are supposed, at least, to believe that there is no such thing as a bad kid. In my school, the nuns clearly believed that certain students were "bad" and through their attitude encouraged other students to treat these kids as outcasts. Woe to the kid who wet his pants, or habitually had a messy desk, or never knew the answer when called on, or couldn't read well. These kids may have been a little immature or genuinely had ADD/AHD or dyslexia, but rather than receiving additional help, they were often ridiculed or treated as lazy or just stupid. Being a poor student was seen as a character defect, or maybe worse. During the height of the Cold War, my sixth-grade nun's favorite accusation to a misbehaving students, along with a wagging finger, was, "You're such a Communistic type."

We learned a variety of things from this. Early on, kids who were treated as bad or inferior soon came to believe it was true. After all, the nuns were authorities and they ultimately spoke for God. For kids who made some early mistakes and were jumped on by the nuns, it became easier and easier to make further mistakes; it was expected of them. There were some mitigations. Not all the nuns were dictators. My first grade teacher, Sister Rosalind, *earned* her reputation as being mean and sharp tongued, but my second grade teacher, Sister John, was a loving and gentle saint. This led to the possibility of a kid's restoring his or her self-esteem before encountering another negative influence. There could be extenuating circumstances at any time, however. For instance, one time while I was standing in line with Sister John's class to go to first communion practice, Sister Rosalind yelled at me and slapped my face because I was talking to the kid behind me.

A kid just didn't know where righteous wrath would strike. When I was in fifth grade, a male lay teacher pushed me down with his foot (I don't know why I was bent over) and knocked my glasses off. He was not my teacher at the time and never was. Like my first-grade teacher, he had a reputation for being mean that was apparently deserved, because he was let go shortly after this. My mother may have contributed to this, because she complained to the school over the "glasses" incident.

Parents were another way a student might get relief from school tracking. If parents understood and had confidence in the goodness of their child, they might stand up against the official and unofficial low expectations of the school. I don't think this happened very often, especially if the teacher involved was a nun. Parents accepted the moral authority of the nuns, and whatever the shortcomings of a nun as an educator, I think parents thought it was somehow sacrilegious to question her. It was telling that my mother was willing to express her concern about a lay teacher. I'm pretty sure she never did so about a nun.

The children who were treated as deficient by the teachers often accepted that judgment and acted that way, largely I think, because it was expected of them. The other kids accepted the official judgment, too, and made outcasts of the "bad" kids. This only exacerbated an already unfortunate situation and denied these children the support and camaraderie of friendship with their peers. Add loneliness to the baggage of the "bad" or the "weird" kids. "Weird," by the way, to us "normal" students, included kids who were extremely pious and the extremely intelligent, who also tended to self-segregate.

Sometimes the "bad" or the lonely kids would form alliances, but they were mostly tenuous and didn't last long. The burden of other-imposed lack of self-esteem is not a very good basis for honor among thieves. One notable exception to this was a boy and girl in my class who were both a bit overweight. This factor, unbalanced by an outstanding personality, was enough in itself to make one's personal value questionable. One reason for this, I'm sure, was the relative rarity of overweight kids (obesity was *quite* rare). The reason for *that*, of course, was all the outside playing we did, including the half hour or so at recess. It surely wasn't from eating low-fat food.

The male part of this odd couple was an affable enough guy. He had a quite laid-back personality and was not the athletic type at all, which probably contributed to his overweight. His female counterpart was also far from physically active, but she was also far from being affable. She actually was a belligerent sort and had a pretty good temper. Somehow, the two of them discovered quality in each other, and it was a match made in heaven (overriding the nuns). I think a lot of the kids sniggered at this relationship at first, but as these two former outcasts found companionship in each other, the consensus was that it was simply sweet. Interestingly, it made the two of them more a part of the social mainstream.

What did you learn in school today,
Dear little boy of mine?
I learned that Washington never told a lie.

Tom Paxton

CHAPTER EIGHT

Lessons Learned

One of the ways of belonging that was prevalent in first and second grade, which surely goes back to the tribal history of all our ancestors, was the gang. We definitely had a gang "problem," and the biggest problem of all was a diminutive kid named Rene'. How it got started I have no idea, but Rene's Gang, of maybe twenty or thirty little kids would thunder around the ten acres or so of playground, running like crazy. Then they'd stop; for what I don't know. I was only marginally a part of the group, so I was never in front where the executive decisions were made. Then, the whole group would rush on to the next stop. It must have looked like a junior version of the Huns sweeping across Europe, and it would have made for a dandy "teachable moment" in history for the nuns, had they been out there.

As I recall, a few alternative gangs were started (everyone wants to belong), but could never rival the original. One might have thought of Rene' as a great natural leader. He certainly could have been a great aerobic instructor! Maybe it was because the gang didn't really do anything except run from place to place, but by third grade, Rene''s Gang was history, Rene' became just another kid, and the gang problem was gone.

***

One of my most poignant memories about school, through the eighth grade, was being left behind or, more accurately, the feeling of being left behind. I don't know about anyone else, but for me, being left behind at school is one of those recurring dreams, like being naked in school or not being able to get a locker open, that made the real incident seem like *déjà vu*. It started with missing the bus. When the second-run bus left, the last students left the school. Kids who rode second-run buses were turned loose when school was done, just as they were at lunch time. We were on our own; it was up to us to be out in front of the school when the bus came around. I can't remember what I was doing, but when I finished doing it and came out to wait for the bus, it was like the Twilight Zone, *I was the only person left in the world.*

I had missed the bus. Fortunately, there was still someone in the school, and I called my mother, who said she would call my father and have him pick me up on his way home from work. This was probably about four o'clock. I figured: My dad probably worked until about 5:00, but probably he would come home sooner because he had a son in distress, so I had about an hour to wait. In way less than that, the final adults left and the school was empty.

The church was adjacent to the school. In the front of the church, at the entrance where my father would enter the parking lot, a broad set of stairs rose up to the church doors. Most of the way up, dividing the stairs into two streams, was a brick half-wall with a flat top and a column on either end, that went up to the overhanging church roof. This was a favorite place for kids to hang out and look out over the parking lot and playfield on the other side. It was a good vantage point for me, so I climbed up on the flat top, which was accessible from the up side, pulled out a book, and sat with my back against a column to read. I didn't have a watch—very few kids had such a luxury, so I could only guess at the time.

When I guessed it was the earliest time my dad might get there, I wasn't concerned that he wasn't; I really couldn't expect him to leave work early, after all. When I guessed it was the time he would be there if he left work at the normal time, I figured that maybe my guess was off, so I allowed for a margin of error of maybe fifteen minutes. When I figured that was up, I began to get a little annoyed, then a little worried. I began to rationalize why he might be late—stopped for gas, flat tire. Then I began to *imagine* why he might be late—car accident, traffic tie-up. What if my mother hadn't gotten through to him? What if he hadn't even been at his office?

Okay, figure this out. If he went home first, *then* came back to pick me up, how long would that take? When the time I figured out had passed, I really began to be afraid. Now, I started to think about going to the convent, across the parking lot beyond the school. That was a frightening enough prospect in itself. I had never been inside the convent or even up to the door. What would it be like? Would the nuns be sitting around in *regular* clothes and be furious that I would see them that way? And what if my dad came while I was inside, and left? If he came back again *at all, he* would kill me! So I waited, and it began to get dark. I became more and more resigned to my fate, feeling ever so much like a martyr (hey, I was in the right place). A spark of hope would rekindle every now and then, as the result of some fanciful explanation, only to be followed by a deeper conviction that I was left behind and I'd have to spend the night there, freezing, and sleeping in front of the church.

And then he came. He had to work late to finish up a job he was figuring, and it wasn't nearly as late as my frightened guesstimate. I wanted to be a little peeved, but, man, I was so relieved!

***

Every once in a while, we kids were presented with the possibility of a "hot lunch." The hot lunch forms would go home (they could print these in great quantity, since the menu *never* changed): the choice of entrée—*one* or *two* hotdogs, side dish—a bag of potato chips, dessert—a little round container of vanilla ice cream, beverage—a small carton of orange drink. We could eschew the orange drink and go with the everyday issue of a carton of milk, but who wanted to pass up an opportunity for something sweet. And, we could carefully mix a bit of orange drink with the ice cream and come up with......well, ice cream mixed with orange drink.

Hot lunch was served in the church basement, which had a fully equipped kitchen and a big open space where tables were set up for kids to eat their dogs and chips. That is, the kids who were lucky enough that their parents had sprung for hot lunch. As I recall, everything on the menu was fifteen cents; so, if you ordered two dogs, a bag of chips, an ice cream and an orange drink, you were looking at seventy-five cents. I have no doubt that this was an extravagant luxury for some kids' families, especially if they had several children enrolled in the school. After all, they already had tuition to cover, and as my dad says, that $120 ($40 each, for three kids) each year was not easy to come by. So, some unfortunate kids only got to look at and smell the hot dogs, something their circumstances in life didn't allow them to have. I am sure that this was character building, and in truth, they didn't miss much. Being in the church basement, however, those hot dogs were sure to have been soul food.

***

My 7th grade nun, Sister Leonita, was one of my favorite teachers. She was unlike any other teacher I had had thus far in my school career. She wasn't mother-like, as Sister John had been in second grade or Miss McGuire had in kindergarten. She was more like an older woman (probably about 30) who was still young and hip, and my pal Ron and I both had a crush on her. That's really saying something; with the exception of Sister John, none of the other nuns could have been described as being lovable in any way. She was very pretty, although it's hard to tell when only a bare face shows under a nun's head gear. None of this is to say that Sister Leonita was easygoing. She actually had a stern countenance and a sharp tongue. But, she was someone we could talk to, who wasn't on another level of being.

That was a complete novelty, and it so appealed to Ron and me that we began staying in the classroom after school to beat erasers, clean the board, and provoke Sister Leonita into a verbal give and take. We would never have attempted such a thing if we hadn't sensed that there was a real and accessible person behind that shroud of dark cloth and stiff white cowling. Instead of hanging out on the swings, waiting for the second-run bus, we decided to spend our time trying to impress our teacher with our innate cleverness.

We were far from being model students. We were definitely *normal* adolescents. That included being curious, a tad mischievous, and increasingly influenced by age-defining hormones. Academically, we both did all right, but we were a ways from applying ourselves fully. But, this wasn't about trying to impress the teacher to improve our grades or to make up for trouble we might have gotten into. We were trying to *recruit* her, in some respects, as an equal and a friend, as someone who understood us. This is usually a rather complicated process with adolescent students and their teachers, since adolescents usually don't fully understand themselves and are looking to their teacher for some clues. The clues I think that we were seeking were that we were lovable and amusing and that we were worthy of love. Evidence of a connection, for us, was making Sister Leonita laugh. I don't think we were ever fully successful, but we did manage a friendly banter that kept both sides amused, and we did evoke more than a few chuckles. For us, such an exchange with an adult authority figure was liberating.

Quite the opposite could be said for "the talk" the eighth grade boys had from the parish priest. This was about---shhhhh—sex. At least we all thought it was; the word was never spoken. Instead, the whole thing was a laughable (and Ron and I have laughed about it many times over the years) exercise in obfuscation and affectation. The affectation was that the priest picked at his nose almost the entire time he was speaking. As for the talk: no one listening to a tape of it or reading a transcript could ever tell, I am sure, that it was about sex--or anything, for that matter. Sister Leonita could have taught that priest a good deal about communication—if nothing else, to have a topic and a point and stick to it. Instead, what we got was one big euphemism, and at that time, for crying out loud, we didn't even know what "euphemism" meant.

***

In the back corner of the church basement was the entrance to the boy's locker room. The locker room itself was actually under part of the school, but the entrance was here. The concrete floor suggested it might have started life as a storage room. It was the *boy's* locker room, because there were no sports for girls. We had a baseball team and a football team. There was no basketball, because there was no gym. There were also no showers in the locker room, only lockers. During football season our kids practiced and played hard--we had a tough coach--so they got dirty and sweated a lot. I'm not sure if showers would have helped the atmosphere in that locker room much, but as it was, it stunk.

What was especially interesting, to some of us guys, about the locker room was that at either end, up about three feet off the floor, was an entrance to the school's utility tunnel. The original part of the school consisted of one hallway with classrooms on either side, and a perpendicular, two-classroom-long hallway in the middle that was also the main entrance. The tunnel made a loop under the school, so the steam line from the boiler room could feed the heaters in each classroom. The tunnel was intriguing to adolescent boys.

There was an undercurrent of talk of mounting an expedition into the tunnel. There were also some primordial fears regarding this. What was actually in there? Maybe some kind of really big, really strange insects or even snakes? What if you got *lost* in there? Or stuck? It *was* awfully low, about five feet from floor to ceiling, and crowded with pipes. And, as tunnel lore would have it, *nobody* had ever gone all the way into the tunnel, or at least no one had come back to tell about it. Tunnel lore also had it that you could see up into the rooms from down there, including the girls' bathroom. *Of course*, the girls' bathroom thing had no particular

55

interest for good Catholic boys, but the whole tunnel thing smacked of a great adventure. Adding to the cachet of it was the possibility of getting caught.

Who would be the Christopher Columbus of the tunnel? Who would risk falling off the edge of the Earth? Who would face the wrath of Queen Isabella (Sr. Domitilla) for failure? It was my best buddy Ron and I, and it didn't take very long to dismiss the analogy to a sea voyage; it was like a desert in there. After all our anticipation, it turned out to be sweaty, dirty, and boring. We had to move along in an exaggerated crouch or on our knees. In some places, we had to climb over or under a cross pipe, and there was the continual danger (and fact) of bumping our heads on pipes. It didn't take long before all we wanted to do was to get the other end, especially after we had made the turn and started back for the exit, some joker turned the lights out. And what about interesting views? What do *you* think? That's how we answered eager questions from our peers about our expedition.

I'd like to think that students at that school still talk about the intrepid explorers who first braved the tunnel. It was talked about enough at the time that it got back to the principal, and we were called into the office. We fully expected to get expelled or, if we were allowed to stay, assigned to beat out erasers forever. As it was, we were asked to consider the stupidity of what we had done and warned not to do it again. And was that a hint of almost-amusement that we detected in the good sister?

***

"I swiped a couple of cigarettes from my mom's purse. Let's go out in the field and try them out." That was my best friend Ron (hey, what are best friends for?). We were in eighth grade, when a lot of stupid kids were already smoking when they could. Cigarettes were easy enough to obtain. Just about every kid's mother smoked, and if a kid could write a note in what looked anything like an adult's handwriting, it usually worked at the corner store. "Please give Jimmy a pack of Camels for me--Mrs. Smith." Or, they were only thirty-five cents in vending machines, even though that was a lot of cash for a kid then. Nobody in our parochial school smoked, at least as far as we knew, but we didn't want to get left behind; we wanted to be just as stupid as our public school peers.

So, out into the field behind the school we went after school. Ever resourceful Ron had remembered to bring matches, and we sat down in the long grass and puffed away. I felt a *little bit* cool, but not much, since there was no one there to watch us. But this little experiment did nothing to answer my longstanding question: What in the world do adults find pleasurable in smoking? The smoke from my mother's cigarettes had always irritated my eyes and nose and made it difficult for me to breathe. Curiously, the moment a cigarette was first lit, I thought it smelled really good; but then, I thought the exhaust from school buses smelled good, too.

Back in the school, we passed Sister Colleen, the other eighth grade teacher. "Have you two been smoking?" My brain started clicking faster than a modern p.c. What were the possibilities here? Denial played out first: She had asked it in more of a suspicious manner than one of moral outrage, so maybe a denial would work. She couldn't really prove anything. Then, something else kicked in: "You can't even think about lying to a religious symbol! That would be a serious sin." Whatever was going on in Ron's brain, I beat him by at least a split second. "I cannot tell a lie, sister. We were smoking."

I don't know if the histrionics were intentional or if the sense of history was conscious, but Sister Colleen was visibly amused and impressed. If I had learned nothing else about history, I'm sure she figured, I knew my young George Washington. She let us go with a mild lecture. Ron was incredulous that I had said what I said, and teased me a bit (for a long time!), but he had to be impressed, himself—we got off scot-free.

***

There were good things and bad things about going to a Catholic school. One of the good things was the development of a strong conscience. Heaven knows we were inundated with dogma on what was right and what was wrong. The effective thing for me, however, especially as a youngster, was the picture the nuns painted of St. Peter writing down in a big book every bad thing I ever did. (I'm sure St. Pete has gotten a computer since then.) If I did it, it was a matter of record, a record that would be checked when I died and would determine (possibly in spite of the amelioration of confession) "where I went" for eternity. That was pretty powerful disincentive to doing wrong.

If St. Peter's karmic scorecard kept me and other Catholic kids in line as youngsters, the arbitrary unfairness of the rules for where "you'd go" led me, and I know others, to do some serious questioning, about the time of adolescence (Gee, imagine that!). Unbaptized babies forever doomed to Limbo was what really got me. I just couldn't see how that was conscionable. Almost fifty years later, Pope Benedict XVI declared that Limbo no longer rocks, and through the circuitous logic religions so often utilize, declared that deceased babies, baptized or not, probably go to Heaven. Finally, the Church catches up with me, the seventh-grade religious scholar.

***

In addition to the "three R's," I have to say that I learned important and useful things in my early school experience that I have applied to real life. I try, for example, to present myself to my own students as a real human being, and make myself accessible for genuine conversation. I try to respond enthusiastically to student humor (even though I don't get the same consideration from my students!). I worked for my contractor dad for years and walked or crawled through many miles of utility tunnels, painting or banding identification onto pipe lines. I always (okay, *usually*) plan to be early picking up people who are depending on me for a ride. I know what they might be thinking if I am late. And I do not smoke.

You just never know when what you learn will come in useful.

***

I recently read *Marley & Me* author John Grogan's memoir, *The Longest Trip Home*. Grogan attended and graduated from Our Lady of Refuge, nine years after I did. He also attended and graduated from West Bloomfield High School, where I went for ninth and tenth grades, before I transferred to Walled Lake High School. The striking difference between his experience and my own, especially in the level of student self-discipline, is remarkable. It just goes to show how much of a wave of change were the first five or ten years of us Baby Boomers as we moved through and made history.

And they called it puppy love

Paul Anka

CHAPTER NINE

Infatuation

Her name was Elizabeth. She had soulful brown eyes, deep languid pools so clear I could see all the way to her pure soul. She was a celebration of softness, with her demur glance and the way she spoke--very slowly, but very musically, like a ballad with not many, but very, very affecting words. She was pretty and shy and gentle. I had been dreaming about her for so long, but just like the Everley Brothers, I was dreamin' my life away. When I first saw her, I was overwhelmed with love; I knew I must win the heart of this perfect woman. But how?

She was nine and I was ten. Maybe I could use my age to my advantage; impress her with my *savoir faire*. Alas, I forgot that girls mature faster than boys. My age did come into play, but sadly not to my advantage.

Elizabeth's family had just moved into the neighborhood from Iowa, into a new ranch house with green cedar shake siding. It was one of the modern breed of homes that were slowly filling in vacant lots around the older-style houses that began life as summer cottages. The last house on the street, a couple of woodsy lots beyond Elizabeth's, was still a cottage, visited only occasionally the whole time I lived there.

Her street was the next one down from mine. A well-worn footpath down the small hill between the two streets was testimony to kids' belief in the utility of the shortest distance between two points. Elizabeth's house was only the third permanently occupied one on the street. An empty lot away from her house and just down the path from mine, was the house of my intermittently good friend Denny. Behind Denny's and Elizabeth's houses was the big woods.

My age became a factor in my courtship of Elizabeth in a couple of general ways. The first was that if this had happened later in life, I wouldn't have been so susceptible to and overwhelmed with love. The thing is, it would have had to come quite a bit later, given that I remained an easy target for Cupid's arrow for quite a while. The second was that if I had been older, I wouldn't have acted so goofy. This, too, took a while to change significantly, considering that I continued to act pretty goofy (though some might change "goofy" to "romantic"), when love struck, for a similarly long time. The fact of the matter is that I acted with Elizabeth just like an infatuated barely ten year-old male. Unfortunately, it played out as a great American tragedy—for me, at least.

This is what happened. Not long after they moved in, Elizabeth and her little sister were in my yard talking with my sisters. I rode up on my bicycle, assessed the situation, and immediately saw a wonderful opportunity to impress the object of my idolatry. I don't remember exactly how I was going to impress her. What I *do* remember is that I ended up running into her with my bike and knocking her down. Oh cruel fate! While my one sister came to the aid of the demurely sobbing Elizabeth and my other sister went to "tell on me," I quickly assessed the situation again. In a flash, I could see that Elizabeth probably wouldn't be interested in true love that day, so I... here I have to ask you to understand that it takes a lot of courage to admit what I'm about to admit, even after all these years...ran. I threw my bike down, abandoned my love in her supreme distress, ran into the house and hid in my bedroom closet.

I don't know how long I stayed in that closet. It couldn't really have been eternity. There was sufficient time, though, amidst the suggestively *hanging* clothes, to play the tape of my bike fiasco over and over in my head. I could see that there was not one molecule of a chance that I could salvage anything that wasn't disastrous out of the situation. "If only I had..." I kept telling myself.

But I hadn't. I was tried, convicted, and sentenced to a life of excruciating embarrassment, self-loathing, and self pity. "Hang Down Your Head Tom Dooley" was a popular song around this time; I knew exactly how he felt. I questioned Justice and the Powers of the Universe, who would let me do something so earth-shakingly stupid. Where were the guardian angels and the good fairies who watched over good kids (Elizabeth was good, even if being very stupid disqualified *me* on this day)?

Justice *was* actually done, but after the fact. Because I was callow enough to run into her in the first place; because I didn't stay, help her up, and apologize profusely; because I ran away and hid, I never won the affection of Elizabeth. In fact, though my heart burned with love for some time, it burned even more from embarrassment. I avoided walking or *riding my bike* past her house, and I avoided her. Then, before I could get over it and maybe reconcile with my darling hit-and-run victim, her family moved out of the neighborhood.

The song with which I will forever associate Elizabeth is Ricky Nelson's "Poor Little Fool." The lyrics are not even remotely appropriate, but this was the number one song about this time, and, of course there is the title, and the refrain "I was a fool, oh yeah." I am sorry, Elizabeth.

***

A few audacious song writers have attempted to sum up love in a word or phrase. "Love Is Blue" comes to mind, and "Love Is A Hurting Thing." Yes, I know that it can also be a "many splendored thing," and I also know that Sonny James had convinced me about this time that *young* love, in particular, was "filled with sweet devotion." In my experience to this point, however, the devotion was all on my side, and the sweetness, as Roy Orbison knew, was "only in dreams."

I was eleven. I was so ready to swim in the sea of love, to have someone put her sweet head on my shoulder. I had tried to connect with a few of the girls in my class; You know, I hung around them, making myself available and being generally obnoxious in order to get noticed. No luck. (Man, I thought girls were supposed to be more advanced than boys at this age—or was that more *mature?*) Sixth grade started, and I was struck hard with infatuation for Sharon.

I needed desperately to know if I had a chance with Sharon, so I decided to ask her. To make it easier on her—well, actually on me—I made it into a multiple-choice quiz. Since I had to wait for the second-run bus, I had access to the classroom after school. I wrote out my little quiz on a small slip of paper: Who do you like best A) ___x___, B) __Chris B.__, or C)___x____? (I'm sure I was B; you're always supposed to pick B if you don't know the answer.) I was going to leave the paper in the cubbyhole under Sharon's desk, where she would find it the next morning. The instructions were for her to leave her answer on the crayon box (she had one of those 64-color mega boxes) at the end of school the next day. I slipped the paper into my shirt pocket to await my chance to plant it.

As fate would have it, I didn't get the chance (or maybe I didn't have the nerve) to leave my quiz of love. It was still there, in my shirt pocket, at the dinner table that night, where my dad noticed it and asked what it was.

"Nothing!" I quickly replied,

"Oh come on; let's see what it is."

This went back and forth a few times. I don't know if my dad was being playful or uncharacteristically nosey and authoritarian, but he insisted that I give the note to him. He started to read it out loud, but I don't know how far he got, because I was off to my bedroom, where I suffered a near-death from mortification experience. I remember someone coming in to comfort me, but the damage was done.

The things we go through for love, or even the hope of love. I never got to find out where I fit on Sharon's list of potential beaus. I guess it was irrelevant, anyway. Until we graduated from eighth grade and went our separate ways, she never showed an interest in *any* boys.

***

The summer I turned fifteen, we moved from the old neighborhood. I had lived there fourteen years, and the neighborhood had changed only a little. There were a few more houses here and there, but its character was unaffected. I've been back a few times over the years, the last time three years ago. As with everything else, change had accelerated, and I literally hardly recognized any of the places that had been the stage for the early acts in my life's play. I was already anticipating change in the neighborhood when we moved, even if I couldn't have envisioned what actually came about. I also knew that I would never forget the wonderful, magical things that had happened to me while I lived there, and I wanted to leave something behind that immortalized them. I wanted something that would say that I had *been here* and had enjoyed it, something some kid not yet born could come across that would make him or her smile.

Two years earlier I had carved a heart into the smooth bark of one of the younger maple trees near the edge of our property. It enclosed my initials and those of my own true love at the time. Even though it was impulsive, I carved it carefully and deeply. I knew that the tree would grow as I would grow, and this would be a symbol of something I hoped would last forever—young love. Does young love ever last forever? Maybe. Maybe. The young love I carved into that tree will go with me to my grave, along with the other loves of my life, and the tree will eventually fall. But there is always *Romeo and Juliet*. It takes me in every time, and every time

I still hope that somehow it will turn out different, happy. Through it and its various analogs, though the young lovers die, young love will, perhaps, always survive.

But is *Romeo and Juliet* credible? In Shakespeare's mind, Juliet was not yet fourteen. She was, therefore, about the same age I was when I fell in love with the girl with whom I shared my carved heart. I *know* that young love can be so consuming, so achingly rapturous, that it could cause someone under its influence to do almost *anything* to honor it. Perhaps it isn't that different from later true love, but young love, that first true love, is not only what it is, it is *new,* an intense pleasure the young lovers never knew existed. And, if it is truly *young* love, it falls upon a tableaux not only of inexperience, but of innocence. There is a much greater chance of its being pure and of its lucky recipients believing that this is all there is, all there ever needs to be, and all there ever will be. Since young love infects the young, though, it's also true that there is a good chance of the young lovers doing something amazingly foolish.

I decided I "liked" Sue (Suzanne) about the middle of seventh grade. "Liking' someone probably has about the same feel to it now as it did then, given the physical and emotional makeup of a young almost-teenager. For me, however, liking would soon enough turn into infatuation and then the complete, beautifully but bafflingly wrapped package of young love.

Can a dream be captured in a photo? I have a black and white snapshot of Sue, standing with four other girls that I took at the field day our school had at the end of my seventh-grade year. They all have on dresses or skirts. Sue's below-the-knee skirt is black with white polka dots. She has on a white long-sleeved blouse, with a small rounded collar buttoned at the neck. Her hair, with long bangs, is turned under with big waves at her shoulders. On her perfectly lovely 13 year-old face is a smile totally innocent and completely captivating. This was definitely my picture of the dream lover Bobby Darin sang about. The fact that I had to disguise that I had found my own true love by asking those other girls to be in the picture, shows that it was still, as Jimmy Clanton put it, just a dream. Six weeks later, that dream came about as close to coming true as I could have hoped.

***

My parents agreed that I could have a party for my thirteenth birthday, in the middle of summer. In the past, having a birthday during summer vacation from school had been a definite loser. This year, it led to one of the most joyous occasions of my life. A good deal of the joy came from the fact that my party actually was a success, something that had been a source of great concern for me right up until the last minute. My school drew from a wide area, in a county where the auto industry had created a wide gap between "haves" and "have a lot mores." A month before my own party, I had attended a pool party given by a classmate who lived in an area of new, expensive homes. It was the same neighborhood where Sue lived; in fact, she and the girl who gave the party were best friends. This was the standard I felt I needed to meet. If I didn't, my party would only serve to emphasize that my family was less well off than those of most of my school friends—not a particularly good way to impress the girl I loved.

The plan was simple, as it had to be. We would walk down to the beach and swim, we would come back to picnic on the massive table my dad had built suspended between two oak trees in our yard, and we would dance in the garage. I scrubbed the garage floor to try to get out some of the oil stains. At least *it* was cement, unlike the ignominious dirt roads that led up to it. We'd have to walk the same dirt roads to the beach. Would my friends be able to overlook my rustic surroundings? Would Sue find me worthy? Would anyone even come?

They came—*she* came. The kids from the newer subdivisions were delighted to swim in the cool, clear lake water with no chlorine. We had so much fun on the walk to and from the lake, who could care what we were walking *on*? We were so famished when we got back, that the grilled hot dogs and burgers were perfection. The birthday cake my mother made was itself almost perfect. There was only one flaw. I blew out all thirteen candles with ease; still, my wish didn't come true. I wished that this moment could go on forever.

The garage could have been *American Bandstand*. All the kids always brought 45's to our parties, so we had the latest and greatest, plus our all-time favorites. We rocked and rolled; we twisted and ponied. But, for me at least, the main point of dancing was the slow dances. What could be more exciting to a sensually naive young man than to feel the body of a young woman pressed, however gingerly, against his own? I danced with Sue, savored her softness, basked in her smile, reveled in her fragrance, and wished my wish again.

We who now have aging parents know all too well the truth that *all* good things must end. I have never experienced that lesson more poignantly than that day. We always capped our parties by playing Dell Shannon's slow and sentimental "Jodie," which was on the flip side of "Runaway."

When the strains of "Jodie" drifted off and parents had regrettably shown up on time to pick up their darlings, my darling was gone. I was sad, of course, but mostly I was numb with the pleasure of a day that had turned out to be virtually perfect.

I guess you'll say
What could make me feel this way
It's my girl.
Temptations

CHAPTER TEN

Young Love

Perfection is so difficult to sustain. Any change renders true perfection less than perfect. Back to school that fall things were considerably less than perfect. Did I sense a certain indifference in the object of my affection? Actually, I sensed a *serious* indifference. Sue was pleasant enough to me, but the whole point of *liking* someone was to treat them as special. Sue was pleasant to *everyone*. This called for serious action. I would confront her. I waited one evening until I thought the coast was clear for this very private operation—not easy when you have one phone, connected to the wall, in a high traffic area, in a small house. I dialed her number. "Hello, Sue? I have to ask you something. Do you *like* me?" My whole world hinged upon her answer. I was taking an enormous risk, but I had to know.

Sue: "No." That was it, one softly-spoken, brutally honest word. I'm sure I remember it precisely. "Okay," I managed to whimper. "Good bye."

It's a good thing the coast was still clear and it was only a short way to my bedroom. It was definitely tears on my pillow time. If she had equivocated, left me *some* hope, it would have been different. But, "No"? How do you rationalize *that?* From that moment on, I would know exactly what Timi Yuro meant by the "Big Hurt."

This was unequivocal devastation-by-love. But things change. After a few weeks of suffering, I rallied. On the playground at school, when there was a group of kids standing and talking, as there usually was, if a guy stood close to a particular girl and she didn't move, it established a connection. I started standing closer and closer to Sue—and she didn't move. Then one day, rapture flashed like lightning across the eighth grade classroom. My last name began with "B," and Sue's started with a "W." In our eighth grade class, I was alphabetically first, and she was last. Since we were seated alphabetically, I was in the first seat in the first row, and she was in the last seat in the last row, as far away as possible. On that rapturous day, I was looking love all the way across the classroom. Sue looked up, caught my eye (and I'm sure my meaning) and flashed "The Smile." It was a lightning bolt that melted my heart and sent a physical thrill through my body. What one word had devastated, one smile restored and renewed.

As inevitably as a romance novel dénouement, we became a couple. Practically, this mostly meant that we acknowledged that the other was very special to us, an affirmation we all need at this time of life. It couldn't be much more; we couldn't drive, and even to call one another was long distance and listed on the phone bill, and, therefore, very much frowned upon by frugal parents. We did have our parties, however, every month or so. (Do kids still have house parties?) In retrospect, it seems as if we had quite a few. The nuns tried to stop these parties, at one point advising our parents that it was not proper for children our age to be commingling socially this way. Fortunately, our parents largely ignored them. Sue, however, only came to about half the parties. Her mother, very religious but fortunately not completely unreasonable, found a way to compromise.

I went to all the parties, but the ones without Sue were more notable for their emptiness than for their fun. It was fortunate, then, that she got to come to Dave's party, over Christmas break. Dave's party was in his bedroom. He had a big family and a small house, but a very large bedroom. It had double bunk beds for Dave and his three brothers. With these pushed against one wall, there was a decent space for dancing. And that's what we did, we danced. If we needed to rest after a few fast dances, we sat on the edge of a bed, talked, and ate some chips and drank some pop. It was high energy fun, but it was also amenable to some serious romance.

Sue wore a tweedy brown jumper with a white blouse underneath. We didn't come to parties in jeans; it was a chance to dress up a little. She was beautiful, and as we danced the slow dances, I said things to her, under the guise of singing along with the lyrics to the song, that I couldn't have said outright. "You are the one love that I adore," and "Whoo hoo I love you, whoo hoo I do. No one could love you like I do." It was heady and intoxicating and gave me the courage to do probably the most daring thing I'd ever done. When the Paris Sisters sang "I love how your eyes close, whenever you kiss me," I pulled my head back slightly, looked at the love in her eyes, leaned closer and closer, and …then I kissed her. It was a passionate kiss. It was a soft and gentle kiss. The passion was in the act itself, not in exaggerating it.

Change is the theme of life, a theme with infinite variations. Most often it's circumstances beyond our control that dictate change. Sometimes, however, we control our own changes. Sometimes we do a good job with this; sometimes we don't. By the time of Carol's skating party in February, I had decided that I didn't want to be "tied down" to one girl. Sue and I had made no commitment—there was no ring, and no promises—it wouldn't have mattered anyway; we couldn't go out with anyone else, because we couldn't even go *out*. What I really had decided was that I didn't want a sweet and lovely young girl to think of me as special anymore. I didn't want the security and comfort of knowing that someone cared for me and wanted to be around me. I didn't want the joy and happiness and exhilaration I had been experiencing for the past several months. So I broke up with Sue.

I should have done a reality check and asked myself: "Are you crazy?" But I guess if you are, you don't think about such things. I made Sue cry, maybe even worse than she had made me cry. Was it revenge I wanted, control, a feeling of power? I don't know, I don't know, I don't know. All I know is that even though Sue and I became friends after a while, we would never again be more than that. I would regret this for a long, long time.

***

At some point in my childhood, Walls Hardware store had opened up next to the Nan's Grocery a mile or so from my house. It had everything from balsa wood and plastic models of cars, planes, and ships to kite string and, I wouldn't be surprised, hardware. I had bought a little pocket knife there, about two inches long. Only a few months after that skating party, having discovered that you don't know what you've got till you lose it, I used my knife to carve my heart into that tree. It was difficult with that little knife, slow going. I had to apply a lot of pressure and be very careful at the same time not to slip and cut myself or mess up the craftsmanship of what I was doing. What I was doing, I knew, was important.

I was admitting to myself that I had been foolish, and I was paying penance for hurting someone I loved. I was declaring to the world that as long as this tree stood and I was alive, I would cherish this love it had been my privilege to share. I was affirming the end of the childhood I had shared with these trees, this place. I vowed that I would periodically go back over this heart, these letters, so that they would last as long as the mighty spreading maple tree that bore them might last. I did go over the carving several times, and before my family moved from the neighborhood I carved it deeper one last time.

I didn't return to that tree for about twenty-five years. Everything had changed, but eventually I decided on the place where it should have been. There was a large tree there—was it my tree? The bark was no longer smooth, but the ridged and cracked bark of a middle-aged silver maple. There were definite scars, however, recognizable especially to one looking for them. The irony was that, as the tree had grown, it had expanded and spread the heart and letters out so that their message was unrecognizable. I decided that the tree had done its job, nonetheless. The love I had left there would never change, but the tree had to grow, as I had to grow. I decided, also, that I had one more thing to do to fulfill my original pledge, so I wrote the following poem.

C B + S W

4-15-62

My tree—her tree—wasn't easy to find
this time.
As our lives have unfolded without connection,
the forest has closed in.
Experience has scored skin variously,
and what was meant to last forever
is disguised by layers of life
Love, once etched
deliberately, impetuously, wishfully
onto smooth skin,
has become an anagram.
Living history is an indulgence
of diminishing returns.

***

"Would you like to dance?" Yeah, it was a pretty common pick-up line, especially when what I really meant was: "Would you care to enter into a

70

devoted, loving relationship, in which you will become the object of my adoration and I will depend upon you for my sense of self-worth and the value of life itself?" It worked, though, because she loved to dance.

Andrea was the most vivacious creature I had ever met. I met her the summer of my fifteenth birthday, at the Green Lake Dance, one of the wonderful summer dances that were regularly put on for teenagers. She put body and soul into her dancing. She was one of those intriguing girls who, being quite overtly religious, are sure of their righteousness. This gives them leave to let their passions run free (within limits, of course) because those passions are born of innocence. I was intrigued, all right--impressed, infatuated, and flattered that she chose to continue dancing with me the rest of the night.

She lived in the neighborhood on the other side of the woods from me, and so went to a different high school than I did. I got her phone number, called her the next day, and walked over to her house. We hit it off perfectly, and my spirits soared. She was beautiful, intelligent, and had a great sense of humor and sense of romance that matched my own. I walked back from her house singing one of the songs from the dance the night before: "Finally I've found my Candy Girl." I was soon to find out that this candy was bittersweet. What should have been an idyllic teen romance turned into matter of prejudice, heartache, and intrigue. You see, Andrea was a Presbyterian and I was a Catholic. Big deal, huh? It was to her mother. After I'd been to Andrea's house a few times, Mom decided that was enough, and she shut me down. But first, there was the birthday party.

I guess summer birthdays aren't bad after all. There was the classic, two years before. Then, the next year, when I turned fourteen, things were looking pretty bleak. It looked as if nobody—and I mean not even my family—was even aware it was my birthday. This was not only the fourteenth anniversary of my birth, but the first anniversary of probably the best party the universe will ever know. I was, as might be expected, blue. So, I did what I typically did with any remotely emotional situation, I picked out a song to be the soundtrack for the occasion.

In this case, it was an almost-hit by Kathy Young, "Happy Birthday Blues," the follow-up to her top-ten "A Thousand Stars." I don't imagine many people remember "Happy Birthday Blues" at all, but it has a special meaning for me. I have thought about it every now and then over the years, and when I recently subscribed to one of those online music download services, I did a search for it. Zowie! There it was. I now can listen to it anytime I want to remember how alone and forgotten I felt that day. I haven't listened to it a whole lot, but it's nice to know it's there if I want to feel bad.

There I was, lying on a seat of our big picnic table, singing "I've got the happy birthday blues" to myself. My mother called me into the house on some pretext or other. When I went back out, whaddya know, there was a cake with candles and a bunch of my friends from the neighborhood—a surprise birthday party, and just what I needed. The party was the idea of two sisters whose family had only just moved into the neighborhood. They had moved from Pontiac, but were cousins of a near-neighbor girl, whom they had visited periodically over the years. I had a big crush on both of them at different times, and Jim and I had hitchhiked into Pontiac to see them one time. Since they had just moved in, the party was a very thoughtful and neighborly thing for them to do. I guess they were the neighborly types; they both ended up marrying guys from the neighborhood.

I don't know how I got to be so lucky, but in my early teen years, when I needed all the affirmation I could get, I had three model birthday parties in a row. My fifteenth birthday was a giant open party—more like a teen dance—at our neighborhood club house. It was joyous, but you'll have to forgive me for forgetting details. Only one thing sticks in my mind. Andrea and I went outside—for a breath of air—and she took my breath away. She taught me how to kiss, I mean *really* kiss.

I don't know if Andrea told her mother we were now kissing, or what, but her mom decided our budding relationship didn't need to blossom. Heavens, it might lead to a *mixed marriage*. I suppose I should have felt preempted by her presumption; after all, it was my church who excommunicated members for marrying non-Catholics. But what I felt was frustration and amazement that someone wanted to erect a wall between two good kids who were falling in love. Ironically, Andrea gave me a book to read, from her mother's propaganda library, *The Wall Is High*, the melodramatically tragic story of a failed "mixed marriage." The "wall" was not that their religions prevented them from marrying, but that they couldn't be Christian enough to get along after they *were* married.

Andrea and I both decided this was pure hooey, and so we began the Year of the Romance That Couldn't Be. She wrote me letters, and going to our mailbox down at the bottom of the Little Hill became a regular ritual for me. I wrote her letters and mailed them at first, but after her mother intercepted one, Andrea asked me to stop. I called her, but if she didn't answer the phone, I could hardly ask for her. If she did answer, she usually couldn't talk, because her wall phone was about as private as mine was. We met at a few of the remaining summer dances, before her mother stopped letting her go. We arranged clandestine meetings at her beach—same lake, through the woods about a half mile from my own. The whole thing was like a soap opera.

Mostly we continued to write letters and found a way other than the U.S. Postal Service to have them delivered. When school started, it so happened that my buddy Ron was going to the same high school as Andrea. I saw Ron once a week, ironically at *Christian doctrine* classes. He became our mailman.

As a Language Arts teacher, I had my students write love letters every year around Valentine's Day. I didn't tell them, but I thought it was a felicitous way for them to develop a capacity to express themselves in writing. It's curious to me, but almost none of my students really got into this. I think it was because someone needs to be actually separated from the object of his or her love by distance, either in miles of by something like prejudice, to appreciate the value of a letter. When notes can be passed to your sweetheart or text messages sent to him or her all day long, the communication becomes infected with inflation. Unlike actual letters, each communication becomes less necessary, less important, and less thoughtful, and its value diminishes. With letters, the greater the distance and the more tragic the separation and the more open, expressive and carefully written the words, the more important the communication is likely to be.

I don't have the letters I wrote to Andrea, but in some of hers to me (of course I save my love letters; don't you?) she makes note of my compelling prose. Compelling or not, it's hard for love to grow without sunshine. By the time we both were old enough to drive, which might have alleviated the situation, love had shriveled from lack of care. There is a happy ending, though. It turns out that I moved and transferred to Andrea's school the next year. She and my future wife were good friends, and we all have remained friends and in touch ever since.

***

My senior year in high school, I started dating Bonnie. Petite, cute and giggly, she was a year younger than I. The song I identify with her is "My Girl," and she was. For the first time ever, I had a relationship I could count on, with no problems or limitations. She wore my class ring. I saw her every day at school, and I could drive the couple of miles over to her house when I felt like it. Her mother was personable and friendly. It was the way love is supposed to be-- sunshine on a cloudy day. It was almost too good to be true.

This went on for a comfortable month or so, and she asked me if I'd like to take her to her junior prom. Would I! I would be delighted to take my girl to her junior prom. My own had been a strange, not altogether satisfying experience. I had asked a girl with whom I had switched schools at the start of the junior year. She was an attractive and personable girl, who had been very popular at her old, my new school. I figured that bringing her to the prom would do wonders for my own popularity. I really hadn't expected her to accept, but she did. *She* had a great time at the prom and at a party later, catching up with all her old friends. *I* felt like the odd man out. Going with Bonnie to her prom could redeem that.

Decked out in my white dinner jacket and bow tie, I showed up early at Bonnie's.

It was s a good thing, because her mother was still fussing over the hem of her sleek white gown. Her mother pinned on her red corsage and my red boutonniere, and we made a lovely couple (I have pictures!). We had a great time at the prom and a fine dinner afterwards. The world was a wonderful place. I felt as if I *belonged* in it, right there, with my fancy duds and my girl on my arm. When I took her home, I kissed her one last, lingering kiss at her door, and it was over.

The next week Bonnie broke up with me and broke my heart. Her best friend delivered my class ring to me at school. Bonnie wouldn't talk to me, wouldn't explain. The explanation seemed obvious, but it was too humiliating, too crushing to accept on top of just breaking up

***

For all its sweetness and all its glory, love is, perhaps more often than not, a hurting thing. We all have to go through multiple heartaches and disappointments before we find "the one"—provided we ever do. Half of all marriages now end in divorce. That's three times as many as in 1950 and twice that of 1966, the year of Bonnie and the junior prom.

Girls and boys still fall in love and break each other's hearts. Is it all worth it? You know it is. Besides, we really don't have much choice, do we?

You load sixteen tons and what do you get?
Another day older and deeper in debt.
St. Peter don't you call me cause I can't go—
I owe my soul to the company store.

Tennessee Ernie Ford

CHAPTER ELEVEN

Workin'

There were always ways to earn money. Admittedly, it usually wasn't much and didn't come easily, but there were ways. The earliest for me started out as pure serendipity. I certainly can't remember the first time, but there was a first time when I found an empty soda pop bottle on the way down to The Beach. Ka-ching!—2-cents bottle deposit. I could trade it in at the Beach House for a Squirrel and a Mary Jane or a Bazooka, or maybe some Chum Gum, and I didn't have to do anything more than bend down, pick it up, and carry it with me. Pop bottles were diamonds scattered around by some good fairy who looked out for good kids. Of course, bad kids found them, too, but I considered myself to be a good kid, so from my perspective it was surely *good* luck.

Sometimes these little growing-up gratuities came easily and conveniently to hand, but pop bottles were like the blackberries that grew here and there along the road. If a kid recognized them for what they were and picked a handful, they were small compensations for being a kid and having to walk along that road. But, to make something really good out of them, I had to get more than one, even if that one was a quart bottle that earned a whopping five cents. To do that, I had to work at it.

75

It was work in more ways than one. Having to walk along that hot and dusty (alternately icy cold and slippery) road was something I had to do to make my enterprise successful. To simply get from one place to another, I could often cut across fields or go through the woods, but people didn't throw bottles out of car windows into the middle of fields.

There *were* compensations for walking the road. There was no end of natural wonders such as a garter snake rustling the leaves in the roadside woods or a box turtle trying to make it across the road without getting flattened by a car. Diversions such as sneaking up on a leopard frog beside a mud puddle or trying to see the woodpecker that was drumming and drilling into one of the trees could relieve the chore of foot commuting. But, when I was deliberately looking for bottles, these things were either not noticed or were distractions. If I wanted to do well, I needed to focus on the task at hand. If I was really on the job, I used a tool adapted from mushroom hunting; I carried a stick long enough to turn over humps in the leaves or grass along the road that might be hiding a bottle. Those fairies had no scruples about making a kid do some of the work.

The payoff with bottle collecting involved a good deal of uncertainty. There was no hourly wage such as the 50 cents an hour I might later on get babysitting; it wasn't even exactly piece work. I was rewarded in proportion to how many bottles I found, but I never knew how many I'd find or even if I'd find any. So, I would sometimes start out for the Nan's Grocery a mile or so away, with no more than lint in my pocket, and develop a mighty thirst along the way. Whether that thirst would be slaked by a *full* frosty bottle of pop, or whether I'd even have the wherewithal to acquire some bubble gum with which to try to work up a little saliva, was always a crap shoot. More than once, I'd drag myself back through the desert, and make it to the home watering hole just before expiring from dehydration.

This was *work* in another way, too. The bottle fairies who looked out for kids were actually the soft drink and beer companies that put the deposits on their bottles to ensure that they'd get them back. Good people (yes, I am making a value judgment) saved their empties and brought them back to the store. But, there were also careless people who eschewed the bottle deposit in favor of the "convenience" of tossing their bottles aside like so many cigarette butts. Whether beverage companies figured that a few enterprising kids would be out beating the bushes seeking the means to a refreshing Push Up or Drumstick, I don't know. I do know that it worked for me—it provided work for me. I was doing my community a service and being rewarded for it.

Did it work for the community? Littering happened on a regular basis, but we kids were like little vacuums where bottles were concerned. By the time my own children were coming of bottle-collecting age in the late 70's, beer and soft drink companies had switched over to cans and no-deposit bottles. Not only did drinkers have little incentive not to throw away their bottles and cans, kids had little incentive to clean them up. There was one mitigation, at least for a while. My kids' school district the two years they went to public school, due to the inspiration and hard work of one very special woman, had started a glass-recycling program and competition with other schools. The school that collected the most glass each month got $100. My kids' school, George Roberts in the Utica, MI district, often came in first and had already developed an interpretive nature trail behind the school with recycling money.

When my kids started at Roberts, I was gung ho for this program and became an active bottle collector once more. Despite the fact that our school was the recycling champs, I could still go out in my pickup truck to nearby roads and make a huge haul. I'd park here and there and pick up, almost literally, tons of bottles. There was one spot where people (I won't otherwise categorize them) would park to enjoy their six packs of beer and bottles of wine. It was a bonanza for a recycler. It was also a part of the shame I began to feel for my fellow human beings who were fouling their own nest.

***

My next enterprise was also road work. My mother was, for a while, the neighborhood correspondent for the Interlakes *News*, the area weekly newspaper, and, I believe, this is how I came to acquire neighborhood "distribution rights" for that same paper. The neighborhood actually encompassed my large subdivision, a smaller one, and several outlying spurs. It was, in all, about five miles of dirt roads, connected by a mile of blacktop. Since this was too much to walk every Thursday, I attached my new paper bag to my trusty one-speed bike, and off I went on my first newspaper career.

I was an independent businessman. That meant I got to collect the money once a month from my seemingly never-at-home customers, whose memories of having not paid were often even worse than mine. Me: "Collect, Mr. Jones—40 cents." Jones: "Didn't I already pay that?" Me: "I don't have it written down in my book." Jones: "Well, you must have forgotten." This kind of exchange would either lead to a customer who was sure I was overcharging him or to some serious damage to my bottom line. Often, I suspect, I didn't make my monthly twelve or fifteen dollar windfall (depending on how many Thursdays there were in the month) This collection responsibility led to my having to knock on some doors almost every week and, sometimes, having customers who were as much as a month or two behind. It slowed down my delivery considerably.

My accounting system, a precursor to my later inability to balance my checkbook, didn't shed much light on this. Since my route passed both the store and beach house, there were sometimes unrecorded costs of doing business. The country store was closer to the beginning of my route, and I usually avoided the temptation to eat or drink up my profits there. The Beach House, on the other end of the route, was another story. In the summer, it was an oasis, not only a beacon, but I'm sure at times a lifesaver from the aforementioned dehydration. There was a risky dependency, here. If it wasn't a collection week, I could be in danger of not having sufficient funds to buy anything but an unpalatable drink of rusty water from the hand pump just down the hill (I swear) from the eight-holer outhouse that serviced the beach area. Here's where my never-ending collection system usually saved me. Since I was collecting from recalcitrant customers nearly every week, I seldom had to even consider drinking from that pump.

That wonderful neighborhood beach is the center of one of my most distinct paper route memories. One summer my aunt and uncle, who lived in the same neighborhood, owned a canoe, which was kept near the beach house. One day, my cousin Joaan (on whom I had a minor crush) and I had paddled that canoe to the other end of the lake—a half mile or so. We were diving out of the canoe and having just the best time, when up popped Thursday afternoon. What a dilemma and what a struggle it was for me to decide to end our fun, paddle all the way back, go home, go get my papers (another mile away), stuff my bag and disperse the news. It was titanic, and it *was* character building.

Delivering papers in summer was often inconvenient and uncomfortable, but winter was life threatening. Talk about the mail going through; I'll bet there were days when the mail *didn't* go through and my papers did. It didn't matter if it was below zero (this was Michigan, remember) or if the roads were snow covered or icy (the snow generally packed down and became ice on our dirt roads). Did you ever try to navigate icy roads on a bicycle? The route had some major hills (it seemed as if it was *all* uphill, but I guess it must have evened out). On icy roads, going downhill was even more treacherous than going uphill.

Cold. Unbelievable cold. What's even more unbelievable is that I apparently never got actual frostbite. Nevertheless, frozen fingers did add to the challenge of making change and not dropping money on collection days. One of the good things I remember about winter paper delivery was doors opening with not only a rush of warm, moist air, but with the almost unbelievably wonderful smell of whatever was cooking for dinner. That, and other smells of cooking wafting from houses as I pedaled past with the dark and cold descending, infused me with the meaning of "home" so intensely that I believe no one could have appreciated it more. This dovetailed with another good thing about winter delivery; I didn't dilly dally anywhere. I had to get home. If I almost dehydrated in the summer, I very nearly starved every Thursday in the winter.

I could count on my mom to save me with dinner on the table when I got home. I could pretty much count on my mom for anything. In the years I had my route, I never missed delivering my papers. It was my responsibility, and I keenly understood that. The one time I had a flat bike tire at the last minute, my mom volunteered to drive me around. This was a little embarrassing, since I prided myself on my stoic responsibility, but the news must go through.

I still had a lot of walking to do, since I put each paper in the door, but I decided that this "motor route" wasn't so bad, after all. Then we came to the Goss's, and their collie-shepherd mix of snarling belligerence. If "Copper" was out, this was the one house where I sometimes threw the paper into the driveway. At that, he would often chase me, and I'd have to hop off and use my bike as a shield. If he wasn't out, I'd go up to the door...but very carefully.

Today, no dog was in sight. I tiptoed to the door. Paper in, and close... but it was one of those doors that makes a clunk when it closes. Instantly, the dog was around the corner in a copper and black whirl. I started to run, but I knew that wasn't going to work. I turned around in a crouch, ready to fight or die. Fortunately, I didn't have to do either. In a heartbeat, Mom was beside me, screaming like a mamma bear and whapping that dog on the nose with a folded newspaper until it beat a hasty retreat.

There are other things that remain strong memories about delivering papers. There was the woman who came to the door in her bra. Whoa! For the times, that was pretty exciting. I never did figure out *why* she came to the door like that. I *did* anticipate collecting there for a while, but I never saw her again. There was the discomfiting novelty of riding the *first-run* school bus, once a week, with the kids from another neighborhood, and getting dropped off to walk the mile home. (It was soooo tempting to take my time walking, since I was getting home "early" and didn't look forward to the task at hand.) I suppose Mark Twain could have written an entire novel based on the things that happened on my paper route. But Mark Twain lived in a different day and age. Actually, so did I.

***

When I was fourteen, I joined a swanky country club. I became a caddy. This departed in some ways from the road work model of my previous jobs, but it still required a lot of walking. Roads did play an important part; I had to get to the country club somehow. Fortunately, there were a lot of drivers going that way, so I walked up to the corner of Commerce Rd. and Green Lake Rd. and stood across from Nan's Grocery and Scottie's Sunoco, stuck out my thumb, and hitched a ride.

I had started hitchhiking a year or so earlier, when I was bored and impatient waiting for that second-run school bus. On a lark, I stood out on the side of Commerce Road that ran by the school playfield and caught a ride. Easy. But wasn't this a formula for disaster—a thirteen year-old boy hitchhiking in front of a school? Maybe it was. We all had heard warnings about perverts of various sorts, and we were wary. Still, a lot of us guys hitchhiked, and it was with our parents' knowledge, if not sanction. I never actually knew of anyone having a problem hitchhiking. But then, those times were a lot safer. Right? Or was it that the news media just didn't play up and sensationalize all the ugly warts we had, the way they do now? I sometimes wonder which it was.

Maybe even scarier, because more real, was the possibility of getting picked up by some "hoods." There definitely was a juvenile (in both senses of that word) social division between what we called "frats" and "greasers." This, of course, ignored the fact that most kids were somewhere in between those poles and didn't necessarily identify with either. Hoods were *bad* greasers, or, I suppose, bad frats, depending on your perspective. Woe to the kid who got picked up by a carload of prowling, predatory hoods. We had all seen their kind in *Blackboard Jungle* and would again soon in *West Side Story*. Good thing the hoods in those movies didn't have cars, or they might have been out cruising the roads looking to pick up innocent hitchhikers to wreak mayhem.

The biggest danger of hitchhiking, it turned out, was not getting picked up in a timely manner. I was a mobile hitchhiker, so I walked as I hitched and often ended up walking most of the way to where I was going. If I had only a mile left, I figured it was probably faster to just concentrate on walking, and I turned on the afterburners on my Keds. Sometimes a driver with whom I had hitched a ride would pick up a second hitchhiker who was only going a short distance (this sometimes happened to me later when I would pick up hitchhikers). It annoyed drivers, as it later annoyed me, to pick up someone who was going less than a mile. I figured someone who couldn't walk a mile was just lazy and gave hitchhikers, and all kids, a bad reputation.

Somehow I regularly survived the dangers of hitchhiking and arrived at the exclusive green of Orchard Lake Country club ready to—sign in. Just because a caddy was there and ready to work, didn't mean he was going to get a "loop" anytime soon. Theoretically, loops were assigned in the order caddies signed in, but members could request a particular caddy or grade of caddy. There were three grades of caddies, "B," "A," and "Captain." To move up from one grade to the next required experience, and members often didn't want inexperienced caddies, so... So, I got another installment of life is only as fair as you make it.

First choice: hang around the starter's booth for a while, rationalize that I wasn't going to get called out anyway, and go home. I could then go down to The Beach and have a good time, but I'd be broke and have to undergo the ignominy of begging my parents for what would ultimately be insufficient funds, anyway. Second choice: Go up to the caddy shack and hope that supply and demand would eventually turn in my favor, and wait for a call down for a loop, meaning a trip around the course carrying a bag. The first of these is the fabled choice of most teenagers—work avoidance. The second is also classic--waiting for opportunity to knock at your door.

Opportunity was definitely present in the caddy shack. Without any effort at all, a guy could discover some of the remaining bad words or behaviors that might have escaped him so far in life. I don't think I need to describe this any further. He also could learn how to create a negative financial balance for the day by spending money at the snack window. The snack window worked this way. After waiting for a while, despite the diversion of the abovementioned vocabulary and experience enhancement, a guy got hungry and thirsty. Understanding this basic human biology (and probably psychology), the country club had food and drink available for the caddies to maintain enough energy to carry those heavy golf bags.

Of course, it wasn't free; otherwise what would be the point of carrying those heavy golf bags? Picking up on the country club ambiance around us, we caddies were exceptionally hungry, thirsty, and susceptible to spending money we weren't earning (otherwise we wouldn't be at the caddy shack).

You might have thought we would have brought our own food—you know, *a lunch*—but that would have been totally uncool. It was far more cool to be hungry, broke, or both.

If the country club ambiance weren't enough to create an insistent appetite, there was the gourmet food. Laugh if you like, but potato chips, Coke, and cream-filled chocolate cupcakes were food for the gods, under the circumstances. Well, maybe not quite. That title would have to be reserved for the toaster-oven sandwiches that were available. I don't know if they're still around, but the brand name was Stewart. To a hungry adolescent (redundant, of course) the smell of a beef burger or ham and cheese toasting was a siren call. You know those cartoons where the character is drawn through the air by his nose attached to the squiggly lines of some wondrous aroma? That was it, and like those cartoons, the door to the kitchen was slammed in your face if you didn't have the price of admission.

That price was pretty steep. As I recall a hot dog was twenty-five cents, a beef burger thirty-five, a ham and cheese forty, and the ultimate submarine or pizza fifty cents.

I was already a veteran of smelling these sandwiches because they had them at our beach house, where adults would buy them, and I would smell them toasting. One of the unrequited desires of my life was to enjoy actually *eating* all of those Stewart sandwiches, but by the time I could afford it, as far as I know, they had disappeared.

Another learning experience available at the caddy shack was playing cards. The card game of choice was acey-deucey (sometimes unimaginatively called "in-between"). Players anted up to create the initial pot. Two cards were dealt face up to the first player, who had the option to bet on the next card's being between them. The bet could be anything up to the amount in the pot. A clever player could figure odds and count cards, putting the odds in his favor, but what I remember most was the enthusiastic "Busted!" from those watching. Getting busted for the pot created exponential temptation for the next player and often quickly led to a pretty big haul for one person and big disappointment and maybe the loss of a day's or more wages for others.

There *was* a third alternative to giving in to labor avoidance by going home or up the hill to the caddy shack. There were several standard (as in "very uncomfortable after a while") park benches behind the starter's booth. A guy could hang out on these and make sure the caddy master knew he was there by asking him a question now and then, maybe even doing little errands for him. Whaddya know, when the next caddy on the list couldn't be located quickly enough to suit the caddy master, the clear and present guy might get the call. I freely admit that I tried all three of these approaches in my years as a caddy, and each had its rewards. You *know* which rewards were the most substantial.

Okay, so I'd finally get a loop. If I'd been nice to the caddy master, I might have gotten one of the nicer, better-tipping club members, or I may have just gotten the luck of the draw. Of course, the member may have gotten the luck of the draw, too. My first time around the course carrying a bag, I was dumb as a brick. I had undergone the standard fifteen-minute group lesson in how to caddy-- and I'm sure it showed. There isn't a whole lot to just carrying a bag, and some members didn't ask for much more. A guy did need to know the basics, such as not to stand between the ball and the hole, how to rake a trap, work the ball wash, watch where the ball landed, and so on. But there were also lots of little and not-so-little things that many members looked for: knowing distances, *anticipating* needs and being in the right place at the right time, having a cheerful disposition, and being fairly articulate.

Experience and good comments from a member moved a guy along the scale from "B" to "A" to "Captain" rating. There was higher pay for each higher grade, and generally better tips. Green as I was, I *earned* my two dollars for that first round. It wasn't much for a good two miles of walking, carrying a bag that might weigh fifty pounds or more (the airline free-baggage limit for golf clubs is, or used to be, seventy pounds). I worked my way up fairly quickly, however, to Captain status and, thereby, had the possibility of carrying doubles (two bags at once) at a rate, with standard tip, of about seven dollars. Two of these a day, which I did occasionally and some other caddies did fairly regularly, would net as much as fifteen dollars, a huge sum in the early and middle 60's. It also netted complete exhaustion and way too much sun.

If you play golf, you know what it's like walking a course on a hot summer day, and I don't mean riding in a cart. Now, imagine (because you probably haven't done it much) *carrying* your bag all the way around and, some days, the bag of another player as well. If you were like me and didn't like to wear hats, all the while the sun would beat down on your head. Even if you wore a hat, the back of your neck would register way beyond well-done on a meat thermometer. With a couple of hours between opportunities for hydration, your mouth would be feeling a little like the Bonneville Salt Flats.

Interim relief, after the front nine, came at the "turn stand," where a microwaved caddy could get a drink of water, sit for a few minutes on a park bench, and prepare for the coup de grass of the back nine. Meanwhile, the golfers would be relaxing and refreshing themselves considerably more lavishly. Most of the time, a golfer would tell a caddy to get something to drink, and there was a little window where we could approach the turn stand. The drink of choice, a mixture of chocolate milk and Vernors (ginger ale) was, to the desert mouth, akin to the whole-body relief of jumping into the lake on a steamy day.

Back on the course, the interim R & R wore off pretty quickly and chocolate milk and Vernors ginger ale was soon a shadowy memory in the sticky coating in my mouth. I could almost hear the back of my neck sizzling like bacon on a grill. The dead weight of the bag tugged mercilessly at my shoulder as I kept adjusting it trying to find a less uncomfortable position. Some of these straps were just canvas webbing and cut into my shoulder. My fevered brain wondered if my golfer had ever actually carried this bag, as I counted down the holes. If he or she knew what it was like, how could he or she expect some kid to carry it?

Then it was over, and callow youth that I was, I had to decide if I wanted to go out again or go home and go swimming. If there was a loop ready to go, I wouldn't have the burden of thinking about it. Otherwise, I'd be weighing things like self-satisfaction at what I had done so far, knowing that I'd only made something like $3.50 for all that hard work, anticipating maybe $7.00 more for a double; and pondering such abstract things as cruel and unusual punishment and compensation for pain and suffering. I'm sure that a lot of lawyers must have once been caddies.

Caddying followed the rule of bottle collecting—if you wanted to make a lot out of it, you had to work hard at it. Some kids, who were more ambitious than I, did make some excellent money as caddies. Besides the immediate pay, at the end of each season, the country club would have a caddy banquet. We caddies were served dinner in the country club dining room, and checks were handed out based on the number of points (awarded for each round) accumulated during the year. These alone could amount to several hundred dollars. Scholarships were also offered through the Evans Foundation, and several caddies I knew got a full ride through college this way.

The caddy banquet Orchard Lake gave each fall was indicative of some of the non-monetary compensations of country club caddying. I got to meet and interact, albeit in a limited way, with wealthy people. I got to witness that they ran the gamut from the good natured—like the guy who would take out a new cigar and ask his caddy, "Do you like music?" and give him the band off his cigar with "Well, here's a band."—to the grouchy and anal, who would throw their clubs if they missed a shot. I can't say I ever got any particular advantage from this exposure, except the knowledge that (these, at least) rich people were pretty much like other people I knew.

Maybe the most luxurious benefit of caddying was getting to play golf on the Orchard Lake Country Club course on Mondays. Mondays, the course was closed for maintenance, but caddies were allowed to play. The very nicest aspect of this was that I brought my dad, a novice but avid golfer, with me a couple of times. Nobody noticed that he was a bit old for a caddy-- or didn't care-- and it was super being able to treat him this way.

A spin off of my country club caddying experience was the opportunity to caddy for professional golfers in two Buick Open golf tournaments. Regional country clubs were allowed to send five of their best caddies to this tournament. This was probably a standard practice around the professional circuit at this time (when top prize money had just risen to $20,000). The word was that caddies got ten percent of whatever their golfer won. I didn't hit the jackpot, here, although one of my golfers had won the Phoenix Open the year before. All of the tournament players now have professional caddies. I don't know what they make, but given the amount of the prize money now, I'll bet the caddies' share isn't chump change. I think I should have turned pro.

You can trust your car
to the man who wears the star.
Texaco gas jingle

CHAPTER TWELVE

What a Gas

I learned, as a caddy, about giving great customer service. It was what separated just hauling the bag around the course from being a competent and complete caddy. This, in turn, generally influenced what kind of tip a caddy would get. I guess it wasn't completely illogical, then, to go from the country club to the service station for my next job, especially since my best friend Ron was already working there. This was the summer I turned sixteen, the summer between going to West Bloomfield High School for two years and transferring to Walled Lake High School for my final two years.

Isn't it funny that the *gas station* serves as a symbol of a major sociological change that occurred in the 1970's? What were "service stations," almost overnight, it seemed, acquired self-serve pumps and charged extra for service. Eventually, there was no service at all, unless you provided it yourself, and "service station" became a thing of the past. The change was economic as well, since it shadowed oil prices going through the ceiling and the rise of discount emporiums such as Kmart and Wal-Mart. Regardless of how the change is classified, service was the victim.

There was a lot of brand loyalty before this. Gasoline credit cards were probably the most common type. There was also fierce competition to get customers to switch brands. Remember all those promotions where different branded stations gave away steak knives or glasses to attract customers? Imagine: gas at a fraction of a dollar, and they were giving things away to get you to buy their gas!

More even than brand loyalty, there was station loyalty. People went to the station where they'd get the best, most friendly, most consistent service. Since service made the critical difference, station owners or managers made it a priority for employees, and for themselves, to provide it. As a child, I would be with my father occasionally when he filled up. He'd always go to the same station, and it wasn't just the Mobil station, it was *Tony's* Mobile. Tony would not only deliver every aspect of service flawlessly, he didn't *ask* my dad if he wanted his oil checked; he just did it. The same went for washing the windows. All the while, he would chat and joke with my dad and generally treat him as a neighbor, even though his station was ten miles from where we lived.

A lot of retail establishments were like that. The scale of things was much smaller, the personal touch was much more important, and customer service was often the deciding factor of who got your business. Neighborly service was the standard, in part because customers were likely to be actual neighbors. But, people would quickly take their business to the store in the next town if they weren't treated the way they wanted to be at the one closest to them. Today, when you get no service no matter *where* you go, you *shop* for gas, and shopping is mostly just a matter of finding the cheapest place for you to fill your own tank.

I worked at the Clark station in Keego Harbor. All we sold was premium gas and oil—and service. My training for the job consisted primarily of how to give good service. Good service meant smiling, being polite, *always* wiping windshield (front and back), and asking if customers wanted their oil checked. It also meant putting air into tires if asked--or better, if a tire looked low, *suggesting* it. For all this the customer paid 34.9 cents for a gallon of gas, a price which didn't go up at all until the mid-70's.

Good service at the Clark station did have some technical aspects to master. It was hard to give fast service, for instance, if I couldn't locate the opening for the gas tank or the latch to open the hood or the oil dip stick (Is this where calling someone a "dipstick" for being dense got started?) The simple thing was to ask the driver, but…well, you know how it is with guys asking directions. Eventually, I became slicker at delivering gas, oil, and service than Goober Pyle. I even gained such esoteric knowledge as that those little Saabs had two-cycle engines, and the oil went *in* the gas tank.

The smile and the friendly service weren't that difficult, even though some customers definitely were. Everyone knows the adage that the customer is always right. Everyone who's had a service job knows that that isn't true, even though the server has to pretend it is. I suppose service station customers reflected the general population in attitude. Most of my customers were pleasant, or at least indifferent. Often the indifferent ones, or even some of the grouchy ones, could be persuaded to reflect my own smile and friendly attitude. Sometimes I felt like a psychologist or a bartender.

There were other times when the opposite would happen, and a customer's apparently jaundiced view of the human condition would rub off on me. It might start with a voice or expression that said to me: "Cut the stupid grin; who do you think you are, Doris Day?" The follow up might be a refusal to be satisfied, no matter what I did, and the worst was if I had actually done something wrong, no matter how small. Customer: "You *missed* a spot on my windshield. Why didn't you wash my mirrors?" Aaargh! "Would you like your oil checked, sir? Here, let me wipe this dipstick on your clean white shirt."

These bumps in the road were usually quickly smoothed out when one my many upbeat customers would come in. One was the fellow who owned the A & W root beer stand across the road, who drove a big, black Cadillac and was the nicest guy in the world. Now and then, he'd give Ron or me a voucher for a free root beer or hot dog. The latter was far from insignificant—that place had the best foot-long chili dogs in the universe! Man, you talk about tube steak! This was New York strip, better than even the *memory* of those toasted sandwiches of yesterday!

Frosty mugs of root beer were the perfect accompaniment for those chili dogs, but the *ultimate* beverage was just a quick walk in the other direction. It was the best-ever chocolate malt from the Keego Dairy Queen. Actually I don't think you could call this just a beverage. A "dessert" needs to be in the description somewhere. Even more to the point, it was an *elixir*. With the first draw on the straw, began a restoration of body and spirit that put the heat of the summer and questions about the goodness of the universe behind me for the moment.

The ambiance of this Dairy Queen, though, involved more than the apparent quality of its food items, because some of the prettiest girls from West Bloomfield High School worked there. I'm sure some of their sweetness affected each one of the confections they dispensed. A chocolate malt was thirty-five cents. You could get a soft-serve cone for a dime.

The smiles from the lovely young maidens? You guessed it—they were priceless.

Another of the characters who frequented the Clark station was the considerably older brother of one of my favorite girls from West Bloomfield High School. She was beautiful, a cheer leader, very personable and very popular. She was also the long-time girl friend of one of the star baseball players, who was a year older and very full of himself. When they broke up once, she accepted my invitation for a date to the local amusement park (no "theme," just amusements), and she asked me to hold on to her boyfriend's ring for her. I was honored…I think. Actually, the whole situation was entirely honorable, and she retrieved the ring and restored both it and her boyfriend before long (sigh!).

Her older brother was a regular customer. He was also a hustler, or at least a wannabe. He held all the high-score records on the pinball machines at the Keego pool hall, which was just a block or two from the Clark station. Pinball was a game of skill, he demonstrated to me a few times. Apply just the right amount of "persuasion" to the machine at just the right time, and you could rack up an infinite number of free games on that first dime. I, however, quickly figured out that, for me, it was also an investment that would require a lot of three-to-a-quarter games to maybe acquire the skill necessary to be a winner.

Pinball, though, for big brother, was passé. The real challenge and the real action were at the pool table and even more so at the card tables in the back room. Since he bought his gas at the Clark station, I would get wind of his windfalls from hints he'd drop and the wads of cash he'd flash. Other times, however, he'd talk Ron and me into lending him a few bucks on his gas credit card, and we knew there was trouble in River City. That wasn't all he talked us into, either. His actual occupation was insurance salesman. He sold both me and Ron life insurance policies that summer.

Buying a life insurance policy at barely sixteen years old turned out to be not such a bad deal. Cashing it in later helped me buy a new furnace for my first house. This same assessment can't be made for the deal Ron and I made with Louis T. Mumalo. Louis T., like our friend from the root beer stand, drove a big black Cadillac,. He also appeared to be a prince of a fellow. He was a "salesman," on the road and short of cash. There was some faultless explanation for this, but I can't remember what it was. Could we lend him $40? The deal was a lot more involved, of course; you don't think we were *that* naïve, do you?

No, he would leave his $300 watch behind as security, and when he came through again next week, he'd pay us back double. But, wait a minute, let's look at that watch. Oh yeah, it's a Longines, with diamonds around the face. Wow! We examined it closely, were suitably impressed, and sent Louis T. on his way with the $40 we scraped together. I'm sure he hadn't gone far before he stopped to take another worthless *Longene* watch from a suitcase full of them so he could be ready for his next stop. Well, we still had a watch. Yeah, it lasted about thirty days before it wouldn't wind anymore.

Pumping gas at a busy station that summer was hot, dirty, and tiring. Since I usually worked with my best friend Ron, we also managed to make it fun much of the time. Contributing to this was the fact that many of our friends from West Bloomfield had recently turned sixteen and could drive, and would stop by for a dollar's worth of gas or a pack of cigarettes. Yes, we sold them, from a big cabinet at one of the pump islands—29 cents a pack-- even though state law said *eighteen* was the minimum age to buy them.

For the first time, I was getting a real pay check, with a week's wages that added up to the heady sum of $50 or so. But maybe the best thing of all was the girls. Omigosh. I grew up in a county with *hundreds* of lakes. Many of them had summer cottages on them where the city folk (read "girls") came to lounge in their shorts and bathing suits. The whole area turned into a resort in the summer. Cass Lake, the county's biggest, was a half mile away from the station, and the extremely popular Dodge Park and its Cass Lake beach were about two miles away.

Between the city and the beach was…the Clark station. Many, many girls, unlike their male counterparts, would stop and ask for directions, which we, of course, we're glad to give, at length. Okay, so we only got to *see* lots of girls, and we could have seen lots more if we had been able to go to the beach and watch them acquiring great tan lines, instead of our just acquiring sunburned necks pumping gas. But, we were learning responsibility! *Right.*

Ron and I did manage to develop a relationship with two gorgeous cousins from the city, whose parents had a summer home on the lake about a mile away. Our pinstriped Clark uniforms probably helped—you know how girls love a uniform! Naturally they would stop to gas up the new black Chevy convertible that belonged to one of them (their families owned grocery stores in the city). A sweet summer romance grew out of this. At least that's how I thought of it. The girls clearly thought of it—as girls are wont to do—as a convenient *friendship*. We spent some quality time with them at the lake and going to some of the really great dances that were put on in the area for teenagers. Then summer was over. I wondered if I would ever see my city girl again. I never did, but she is immortalized for me in Robin Ward's song "Wonderful Summer."

***

Many years later, I taught a community college introduction to poetry class. One of the poems I became very familiar with was Elizabeth Bishop's "Filling Station," which was written the same year as my first summer working at the Clark station. What seemed to me to be the poet's condescending attitude towards people who work at service stations contrasted so greatly with my own experience that I wrote an "answer" poem to share with my students. You can read "Filling Station" at *http:// californiapoet.blogspot.com/2010/08/elizabeth-bishops-filling-station-word. html.*

You can read my poem here.

FULL SERVICE

I guess you had to be there, as I was summer '65,
when the Bishops, Fords, and Princes in their Lincolns would arrive
at the stations of life, where "service" was taken literally;
some of us provided, others expected, all quite naturally.

We worked for wages, such as they were, an occasional tip, and pride
in a job well done and purposes filled, feeling good inside.
We were almost human, a poet averred, but her self-serving vision
digging dirt ahead of her time, requires critical revision.

We were loved, it's true,
your patron's insight was correct.
But you didn't quite see that we gave love too,
did more than just collect.

CHAPTER THIRTEEN

I Get Around

There was the Big Hill and the Little Hill on Woodview. They lay between my house and The Beach, so they were essential landmarks. Between them, they embodied a goodly number of life lessons. The first of both of these was perspective. From an adult's perspective, only one of the hills was aptly named, the Little Hill. It was maybe thirty feet long with about a twenty percent drop. It was just enough to create rivulets of water when it rained, so we kids could make elaborate systems of canals and lakes in the sandy side road at its base. Since there were no houses on this one-block spur and almost no traffic in our end of the neighborhood anyway, we could play here at being a junior Army Corps of Engineers to our hearts content.

Today was dry, however, and the road down the hill was packed hard and embedded with stones. I had been teaching myself to ride my big sister's bike, hopping on with a running push and seeing how far I could go before I lost my balance and had to bail out. If she hadn't had a *girl's bike* with no stabilizing central bar across the top, I thought I could do better, although I probably couldn't have reached the pedals. As it was, I was getting it and was able to make sizeable, if wobbly, hops down the road.

But now, I was coming to the Little Hill. Yeah, I knew it was there—it was only about fifty yards from my house—but I was daring myself to ride a bike down it. Then the crest was there. I had to make a quick decision: Go down it or not; risk my young life or not? I went for it. But I hadn't accounted for acceleration and its exacerbating effect on wobbling

93

handlebars. Bike wheels that turn so smoothly parallel to the road don't like to be jerked sidewise. Gravity trumped inertia, and down I went. Ouch! I had also not taken into account the effects of friction and the difference in resistance between the road surface and the skin on my shin.

My mom patched up my bloody leg, and before the scab was gone, I had conquered that hill. I was ready for my own bike. As far as I remember, there were two sizes of bike available at this time, 24" and 26". There were none of those mini-bikes of my son's generation, with the high handlebars and banana seats. There also were no mountain bikes or BMX bikes. The only alternative to a "bike" was what we called an English racer, the kind with thin tires, skinny little seats, multiple gears, and caliper brakes. All of the bikes in *my* neighborhood had regular tires, saddle seats, one gear, and braking that was done by pedaling backwards.

My dad found a used 24" bike for me somewhere, and we fixed it up. That meant that we sanded off some of the rust, oiled the chain, and painted it. My dad, the painter, could fix anything with a coat of paint. I'm sure he possessed greater fix-it skills than that—things did somehow get fixed-- but that's the basic lesson I learned from him. I'm still far from a whiz at fixing things, but I can usually make things *look* good with a coat of paint.

Riding my new bike was a new challenge, but having my own bike was also a new motivation. The crossbar of a boy's bike was daunting, since its limitation caused my feet to barely reach the pedals. By putting the seat in as low a position as possible, though, I was able to make it go. Before long, I was more or less ready for the Big Hill, which in actuality was only a less small than the Little Hill. Nevertheless a monster from a kid's perspective, it was another fifty yards or so down from the Little Hill. It was probably four times as long and twice as steep as its smaller counterpart. The biggest challenge to the Big Hill, I soon found out, was pedaling up it. I couldn't do it. Since my legs were too short to push the pedals all the way down efficiently without severely compromising my crotch, I couldn't overcome the incline. To create torque, I had to lean way over to one side, push down, then lean way over to the other side and push. This was not only inefficient, it was awkward and tiring. Coasting down, although a little scary, was not that big of a problem, but I had to get off and *push* my bike to get up the Big Hill until my legs grew a bit more.

***

I wonder how any *millions* of miles I rode on my various bikes. I eventually got a new 26", and then, I think, one or two others. These were always the $39 special at Western Auto or Wards, and had to face the challenge of the rough use I gave them on our dusty, bumpy roads. Maintenance consisted of oiling the chain, tightening the handlebars, and a very occasional washing. Field repair resulted from the annoyingly common chain jumping the sprocket. This could usually be accomplished by threading the chain back onto the sprocket with one hand, while pushing on a pedal with the other, if the chain was loose enough. Oily, gritty hands from this operation gave testament to how much sand was mixed with the oil on the chain. What our bikes lacked in sophistication, they had to make up for in durability.

One thing that was almost never a problem was bike theft. We'd ride our bikes to point A, drop them to the ground, and go off to do whatever we came to do. Even with the sometimes dozens of bikes abandoned near the entrance to The Beach, often left there for the better part of a day and never with a lock, there was almost never a missing bike. Very occasionally, some kid would take a bike and use it for a while, but they were never stolen permanently. I don't know if this was a result of strong ethic against stealing or just a recognition that every kid's bike was easily identifiable. We didn't have to worry much, however, about bikes riding off without us..

Bikes were truly multi-purpose vehicles. Mine was for straddling, with tiptoes on the ground, while I shared a conversation with friends-- especially girls who I would *like* to be my friend--in the middle of the road or in a parking lot or yard. It was for going out to eat, when I just *had* to have an ice cream or bag of chips. It was a commercial vehicle, used for my paper route. It was a pleasure vehicle for cruising with the wind in my face. Maybe best of all, my bike was a proto-space shuttle for exploring the space anywhere outside where I'd been before, even if I'd been by it in a car. The range was limited only by how far I could get in half the time I had to be out—I had to come back, too.

When I got old enough and brave enough to take my bike beyond the dirt roads and onto the pavement, it was both a revelation and a liberation. The revelation was that it was so easy to ride on blacktop and I could go so fast. The liberation was the expansion of space that became my territory. With this newfound freedom, came new responsibility, of course. The real-world bicycle-riding rule of the road for highways, as I saw it, was not to slow anyone down. This meant switching sides of the road when traffic was coming ahead or behind on the side of the road I was on. It involved quick looks over my shoulder and timing that could be a little tricky. The resulting lane weaving could be very disconcerting to car drivers, and every once in a while one would honk or yell at me. At the time, I considered this a little ungrateful, since I was just trying to stay out of their way. When I learned to drive, I understood the drivers' anxiety over bikers who were unpredictable. I also figured out that I was lucky I was never run over by a driver pulling out to pass me just as I was switching into the passing lane.

The *quality* of the new territory opened to me by highways wasn't that different, but it still felt as if I were experiencing more of the real world. It was a more leisurely and close-up version of going for car rides around the area with my parents and provided an expanded perspective on the everyday life of my extended neighborhood. My buddy Jim and I, before long, devised a series of "bike hikes," to take fuller advantage of this. Jim's older brother had been in the Army, so Jim had a real canteen that at least kept us from total dehydration on these jaunts. That usually was the extent of our supplies—we weren't very good at planning—and we rarely had much, if any money between us. We biked into the towns around us— Milford was the farthest, about fifteen miles.

The best trip, however, was to the Pontiac Airport, about ten miles away, with an atypically planned-for stop at the nearby Richardson Dairy for a sustaining ice cream cone. The airport was high excitement for kids whose primary interaction with planes was watching them drone across the blue sky while lying on our backs in the grass. Jim and I rode our bikes into the airport and over to the hangars, where we got to look at planes up close and talk to some pilots and mechanics.

Unfortunately, there were no jets at this airport, but there would have been no jets if this had been the Detroit or New York airport, since passenger jet service wouldn't start anywhere in this country until later that year. There were plenty of military jets *in the sky*, however, since we were only about thirty miles away from Selfridge Air Force Base. Jets obviously would have been our choice to see, since when we imitated aircraft as kids, it was with our arms out diagonally behind us and with the roar of a jet, not the drone of a plane. Still, seeing all the planes taking off and landing was cool, and we were happy. We were also pretty tired by the time we got home and told our pretty *un*happy mothers where we'd been.

Jets definitely represented high technology and adventure. We saw them do their thing at the movies, and probably every boy (and no doubt some girls, too) had at least one plastic jet that he had glued together from a model kit. (These were the days when "airplane" glue was used only for assembling models.) The other place we typically saw them was as a bright point of light in the sky at the head of a long vapor trail. Once in a while, one would streak by low enough to clearly see its shape. The roar from one of these would roust a house full of kids outside to sweep the sky faster than a crew of anti-aircraft gunners. The more usual low-flying aircraft were lumbering C-130's or an occasional helicopter. All of these aircraft were reassuring symbols to us of the military might of "our side" in the Cold War. At the same time, they were a little disconcerting, one of the frequent reminders that the world might get blown up at any minute in a nuclear holocaust.

Mass destruction from a Soviet nuclear attack was the cause of almost universal anxiety at this time. A fallout shelter was the only, albeit pitiful, protection the common man might have from atomic extinction. My parents were neither anxious enough nor well-off enough to buy or construct a home fallout shelter. My school had only a basement, and that only under the church and not the school itself. There were drums of "civil defense" rations in the locker/storage room down there, but no actual fallout shelter. We did, however, have drills on how to get under our desks if there was a nuclear attack. The joke going around was that you were supposed to bend over with your head between your legs as far as you could go and kiss your ass goodbye.

That pretty much summed it up. If there were a nuclear war, we all knew that it was the end of the world. This never seemed more real to me than when I read a "doomsday" book in 8th grade called *Level Seven*, which ended with "Our father, who art in Heaven..." as radiation overcame the last man on earth. This was followed by *On the Beach* and *Alas Babylon*, which were far more deeply terrifying than all the graphically detailed horror movies that would become increasingly popular in the coming decades.

Thus it was that Jim and I went on a bike hike in search of the Nike missile site that was reputed to be near us. Given the recent launch of Sputnik, anything like a rocket was cutting edge stuff. We didn't know exactly where the Nike site was, but we eventually found it, out in the boondocks on a dirt road. Exciting it wasn't. The only visible evidence it was even there was a high grassy berm topped by a barbed-wire fence, a sign, and a guarded entrance gate. Needless to say, they didn't let us in to look around. Not that we asked or even hung around that place. Either one of these, we figured, might put us under suspicion of being spies.

CHAPTER FOURTEEN

Car Talk

Since we were a one-car family until the early 60's, use of the car was primarily limited to my father's going to work. If my mother wanted to go shopping, for example, it would have to be after dinner or on a weekend. (It should be noted that neither my mother nor anyone I knew "went shopping," as such. Shopping wasn't recreation; shoppers went to buy some particular thing.) Friday night, my mom would usually go to the grocery store—along with half the rest of the universe who had just gotten their paychecks. If my dad went along, I'd usually sit in the car with him while my mother went in. If I did go in, I could never wait to get to the meat and fish departments.

In meats, I loved to look at the cow tongues. My mother actually bought one a couple of times, and sliced, it made quite good sandwiches. It didn't taste just like chicken, but it did taste just like beef. The other thing that both fascinated and repelled me were the sweetmeats, a.k.a. sheep brains. My dad was always ready to testify that "fried brains" were a special treat, but I have never known him to actually *eat* any. In fish, I was always fascinated by the variety and size of the whole fishes in the case This was confirmation to me that there actually were fish over seven inches long, which was the longest I had I ever caught. I have to say, though, that my little fish were the only fresh ones we ate, since my mother only ever bought frozen fish sticks. Come to think of it, those were only seven inches long, too.

Shopping for most anything besides groceries meant going to downtown Pontiac to one of the department stores or to the five and ten cent store, Kresge's. I can remember being very concerned about the sparking of the street cars where they connected to the overhead wires. I also recall a policeman or someone else with a loud speaker, up in one of the buildings, chastising people for jay walking. I remember sitting with my dad in the alley behind the Federal Department Store one night, waiting for my mom and listening to "Sixteen Tons" on the radio on WJR, "the Great Voice of the Great Lakes." From the parking lot of a grocery store on the edge of Pontiac nearest us, I could see the fascinating high-tech sign at the Vernors Ginger Ale plant. At night, the neon would light up sequentially to make it look like the giant Vernors bottle was pouring out its contents and filling a glass. Then, the glass would empty, and it would start all over again. I would have been content to sit parked there waiting for my mom to shop and watch that thing for hours.

The most frequent recreational use of the car when I was a kid was the "rides" we used to take. "Who wants to take a ride?" my dad would call out on summer nights. There was never any shortage of takers. Then, we'd ride around the area, seeing what we could see. It was a great way for my parents to relax, to talk quietly in the front seat and not to have to worry about us kids. For us kids, aside from a "few" disagreements over who was impinging upon whose space, it was also a great way to unwind after a hard day playing outside. Talk about inexpensive entertainment; with gas at less than 30 cents a gallon, we could cruise all evening for less than a dollar.

Going for a ride was also educational in a real-world way. There were lakes all around us, and the neighborhoods varied quite a bit in style and wealth. I became aware very early of the social and economic strata of the world. We also were never more than a few miles away from the "country" with its barns and rows of corn or beans, and horses, cows, or other animals. It really gave us kids a sense of what kind of a place we lived in that we never would have gotten by staying home or just going to school. It was interesting, too! I never tired of looking out the window and seeing, hearing, or smelling the character of the places we'd pass.

The ultimate reward was that this ritual often ended up with stopping for an ice cream cone. My dad knew all the places, though we had regular spots, too, the Dairy Depot in Union Lake being our favorite. If we went as far as Milford, Capes Ice Cream, which made its own, was fantastic.

The ice cream was piled high in those days. It really put to shame those expensive, billiard balls stuck onto the chain-store cones of today. It was also literally *creamy*, full of unhealthy butterfat that mysteriously never seemed to affect any of us. Well, that's not exactly true; the effect was that it tasted delightful and made us all very happy. Cooled off and otherwise satisfied by a pistachio (my favorite) or strawberry or butter pecan cone, and with the Michigan night temperature dropping off quickly, we kids would put aside our territorial prerogatives and huddle together for warmth. We often arrived back from our ride sleeping peacefully.

Another recreational use for the car that also often ended up with sleeping children was going to the drive-in movies. I'm not sure why drive-ins fell into disuse; they were truly great multi-purpose establishments, especially for families. They acted as babysitters for younger children, who, after playing on the theater's playground equipment before it was dark enough to start the movie, would find it hard to keep their eyes open far into the movie. Double features were the standard, and even if my parents had to put up with us kids bugging them to take us to the refreshment stand to use the bathroom, it was a long time before we could last long into the second feature.

We seldom used the refreshment stand for refreshments. Instead, my mom would pop enough popcorn to half fill up a grocery bag and make thermos jugs of kool aid. I always wondered what those Flavos Shrimp Rolls that were advertised during intermissions were like; I never did find out. After returning from the refreshment stand, the favorite way of making the time between movies pass quickly was holding our breaths. There was a clock on the screen that ticked off the time remaining, and my dad would challenge us to see who could hold his or her breath the longest. He was always the champ; his record was four minutes.

***

Two or three times a year we'd drive to Ohio to visit my grandparents, aunts and uncles, and cousins. The trips when we were small were the best. It was at least a six-hour trip on two-lane highways in those days, and we'd always leave after a quick dinner on Friday night. My dad had bought a used 1946 "woody" station wagon from someone in the neighborhood. We kids would be in our jammies with plenty of blankets in the back cargo space, and we would have an absolute blast "sleeping out" back there. At roughly ten-minute intervals, however, one little voice or another would call out, "I gotta go. Really *bad*," and my dad would pull off onto the shoulder. At night, along those two-lane roads, there were no rest areas or much of anything else. But my dad was prepared; he always had a clean one-gallon paint can with the rim cut out. If you just couldn't wait, it was down with your drawers on the side of the road, and pee in the can. Then he'd dump it out. Why the can? Hey, we weren't *primitive*.

There were several different highways we could take to Dayton, and my dad would switch off, trying to find the best route. One led us under a massive concrete railroad bridge over the road. I don't know how the story got started, but while building this particular bridge, a worker was supposed to have fallen into the wet concrete and was entombed in the bridge. With virtually every concrete bridge we went under, we kids would want to know, "Is that the bridge with the man in it?" I'm not sure why he did, but after a while and much to our disappointment, my dad stopped taking that route altogether.

***

We would also use that station wagon to go the other way, "Up North." Everyone went up north--anywhere north of Midland, Michigan. Just about everyone, it seemed, also had a "cabin" up north or knew someone who did. It's a great testament to the effectiveness of Michigan winter that the northern part of the state wasn't and isn't overpopulated. My oldest memory of going up north was in that woody wagon. By the time we arrived, everyone was quite ready to hit the sack. We went into the cabin (rented or belonging to some friends) and all of the floors were covered with dead flies. I guess my parents swept them up; that's all I remember. I conked out, flies or no flies.

Later on, my parents became good friends with a couple, the wife of whom had been born and raised in a huge log cabin near Grayling. She had fifteen brothers and sisters. None of them lived in the old house anymore, only the mother, who was tiny, bent over, and always wore her steel-gray hair up in a bun. Her name was Bessie, and she was heroic.

The log-cabin home Bessie presided over had nine bedrooms—one down and eight up, one giant fireplace in the cavernous living room, and a mess hall of a kitchen. In the kitchen was a large wood cook stove and a long, long table made of wood planks, with benches the same. At one end of the kitchen was the water system, an artesian well of ice-cold spring water that filled a 55-gallon drum and overflowed via a little pipe into the large white sink. A memorable part of our visits were the flat and absolutely delicious pancakes Bessie would make for the masses in residence on summer mornings. These would often be studded with wild huckleberries that we kids gathered when we were there.

Oh yes…and there was also a two-holer out in the back.

This may have been the most perfect place possible for kids to go up north for a week every summer. The cabin was just up a low meadowed hill from the North Branch of the Ausable River, one of the prettiest in the world. Its cold, crystal water was the source of never-ending interest and amusement, including a kind of "swimming" that was novel for us lake kids. One of the adults would drive us miles upstream and we'd float down on inner tubes. Or, we'd walk down from the cabin, get in, and let the swift current carry us along for a way. Then, we'd get out, walk back up stream, and do it over again. We'd wear old shoes and leave them on in the water to protect against the rocky bottom, but in spots, the river bottom was clay, polished smooth by the racing water. In these spots we could stand and slide along the bottom as slick as if it were ice.

At night we'd play tonk or Michigan rummy, both of which accommodate at least eight players. Later on, the older boys would amuse themselves by using snowshoes to bat the multitude of bats that would cruise the open, roofed porch on two sides of the house. It was long before video games and involved way more physical exercise, if not more hand-eye coordination. In fact, though it was reputed that the older cousins were quite proficient at "batting bats," I never saw anyone hit one.

One of the special interests of this summer place was the proximity of the Michigan National Guard Camp. Michigan shared this camp with other state national guards for training exercises in the summer. Some of the older cousins, up for the summer, would wait until one group had finished its training and returned home, and then go search the training area for leftover ammunition or equipment. I'm sure this was extremely dangerous, but they had been doing it for years. One of the years we were visiting, they had found field telephones and miles of wire left behind. With these, they connected eight of the local phoneless cabins into their own telephone system.

I went out one misty morning with the big guys, looking for stuff. Fortunately, most of what we found were dummy mortar rounds and spent BAR casings. We did find a number of live regular and tracer BAR rounds, which the older boys kept to use in their own 30.06 rifles. What I got was a ton of spent casings, and a bunch of ring clips that fit together to make bandoliers, like Pancho Villa's. Threaded through a notched-out "machine gun" I made from a piece of 4 x 4 and some pipe, these were terrific for playing war with my buddies out in the old apple orchard back home where we picked wild strawberries.

***

The summer I worked at the Clark station, I bought my first car. It was a beauty: a blue and white 1956 Pontiac Chieftain, that ran great and had a clean interior right down to the woven plastic driver's seat pad and hardly any rust. It cost an entire week's pay, $50. I have to tell you right up front that the story I'm about to relate is of a great tragedy: *Reader discretion is advised.* You see, I loved that car. Sure, I'd only had it a short time, but we were intimate. Hadn't I washed and waxed her outside and scrubbed the fat white walls? Hadn't I vacuumed and cleaned the inside and washed all the windows till they sparkled? I did, and I had her ready to go! Then, why oh why, I'll always want to know, did I have to run into that tree?

You're getting the picture; this is another embarrassing story of me, being dumb. That makes it really hard to tell, but, you know, I learned a big lesson, and I feel I ought to pass it on Actually, I'm still indulging in self-flagellation; I'm still p.o.ed at myself; I deserve to be embarrassed. I surely wish I had that car back now. I know, I could buy another one--for fifteen or twenty thousand dollars.

This is what happened. I had just gotten my driver's license, and I badly wanted my own car. I found out about the Pontiac for sale by some older, single guy, who worked at Pontiac Motors and was ready to buy a new one. I went to look at the car—only a few blocks from the Clark station where I worked, loved it, and made a deal with the guy. I gave him ten dollars and told him I'd bring the rest on Friday, when I got my check. Man, my spirits were soaring; I could hardly wait. My own car!

After I picked up my new ride, I took her home to make her really mine. I spent all day Saturday getting that baby lookin' good, ready to roll. I was pretty worn out, but my adrenaline was pumping overtime, and Saturday night was calling. I got *myself* cleaned up and duded up, and I was ready to go show off my wheels. Never got there. Even though we had moved, we still lived on dirt roads about a mile from the highway. There were washboard bumps in places on Halstead Rd. heading for Pontiac Trail, and there were intermittent trees along the side. Down the road, comes a callow sixteen year old, steering the car with his knees. . . (*Last warning—this gets ugly.*)

Not long before I started working at the Clark station at the beginning of the summer, my buddy Ron had taken up smoking. I, having at least as high a need-to-be-as- cool-as-possible quotient as he did, decided I'd take it up myself. Before long, however, I figured that smoking a pipe would be even more cool, so I bought one and some Cherry Blend tobacco. On the evening in question, I set out, nattily dressed in my Jack Purcells, my Levis, and especially my madras cotton windbreaker--the height of fashion as I saw it. To complete the picture, I had to light my pipe. So you see, that's why I was steering with my knees, when I hit that washboard and the car veered into that little tree on the roadside. I was, of course, trying to light my pipe. *(I told you it wasn't pretty.)*

I walked back home, talking unkindly to myself, told my dad what had happened, and faced the consequences. Fortunately, I suppose, this was not unfamiliar ground for me. I was already inured to being painfully embarrassed and devastated by some stupid thing I'd done. Still, I *was* painfully embarrassed, I *was* devastated, and I didn't get to go out that night. My dad and I went to look at the car, quickly decided there was considerably more than fifty dollars worth of damage, and called a wrecker to come and haul it away. Its value as junk cancelled the towing cost, and that was that. My car was gone, just as if it had never been there.

The effects carried over, however. I felt such grief over the car I had so enticingly barely had, that I had to have another one. I saved my money and bought a '59 Pontiac Star Chief. This car cost a heady $100, and it was BIG, a plus factor for hauling around a bunch of my friends. It also had a monster V-8 engine and would have been pretty fast, despite weighing tons and tons, except that the engine had a burnt valve. If I stepped on the gas with anything more than a gentle touch, it would go "pop, pop, pop" and there would be no power at all. The other effect of this was that I could almost see the gas gauge slide toward empty as I drove. Even with regular gas at 29.9 cents a gallon, this was an expensive beast to drive.

The privilege of driving to Walled Lake High School, instead of the ignominy of riding the bus, was highly desirable, however. The downside was that I was on the Walled Lake wrestling team, and practice had begun. I drove straight to work after practice. I had to keep working at the Clark station in order to keep my rusty-brown beast in fuel. It soon became apparent that I couldn't keep going to school, wrestling, working, doing my homework, and still have time to sleep. Much to my everlasting chagrin, I jettisoned wrestling (I didn't do so well with the homework, either).

I suppose the recent research findings on teen brain development, or more accurately *lack* of development, account for much of my own teenage behavior with relation to moving vehicles (what I've put down here certainly isn't a comprehensive list.) While it may help to explain my behavior, it doesn't much excuse it. It doesn't restore my '56 Pontiac or get me a varsity letter in wrestling.

***

Up to the time I got my driver's license, I would often listen to Lee Allen's radio program on WXYZ 1270. Each night he would sign off with: Watch how you drive that car of yours, and don't you dare turn it into a couple of tons of deadly weapon." I'd like to think the most popular deejay in Detroit had a lot of influence over kids and prevented a lot of car crashes. In my case, however, it was mostly luck that prevented the teenage me from the tragedy of doing just the opposite of what Mr. Allen exhorted nightly.

'Tis the gift to be simple,
'Tis the gift to be free
Simple Gifts

CHAPTER FIFTEEN

Simple Gifts

I was watching a gaggle of my grand nieces and nephews play all out and full speed ahead at the big backyard reception for their aunt's wedding. They giggled and squealed and called out. They challenged and chased or retreated, changing roles in an instant. I knew they would continue having their fun until they almost literally dropped in their tracks. I knew this, because I saw myself out there, quite a few years before.

I was chasing around the vast church hall with my own little cousins after my Aunt Irene & Uncle Dean's wedding. I was four years old, it was my very first wedding, and I was dazzled by my aunt in her snowy dress covered with crystals of frosty lace flowing into a snowslide of train. My uncle's midnight-black tux was equally splendid, and together they were the vision to me of a prince and princess. I was also dazzled by the biggest, whitest cake I had ever seen, with its prince and princess in court on its towering top. I wanted some of that cake in the worst way, but for now I was completely committed to running and giggling with my cousins around that hall--until I found it impossible to keep my eyes open. . .a. . .second. . . . longer.

My aunt and uncle's wedding was special-occasion: continuous, runaway, run-till-you-drop fun. Everyday fun could be like that at times, but mostly everyday fun came and went like scudding clouds on a breezy summer day. Fun came in every size and shape imaginable, from rubbing a dog's belly until one of its back legs made wild scratching motions, to stringing dandelion stems together to make a necklace, to hunting squirrels with a bow and arrow. The thing is, brief though it often was, it was always around in one form or other and to some degree or other.

Even mornings had their breakthrough rays of sunshine. Take the reading of cereal boxes, for example. The quality of the experience ranged considerably, but cereal manufacturers understood that kids often needed and enjoyed having something to jump start their morning brains. If it was entertaining as well, so much the better. Something to read on the back of their boxes was an essential part of their product, and it helped to sell it. For a while, one manufacturer, Chex I think, actually printed a sort of community newspaper on the back of their boxes.

A bit more fun would be something bright and colorful on the box that made me smile or maybe laugh—a cartoon perhaps. Better, was a giveaway packed inside and emblazoned on the box, both back and front, that made me beg my mom to buy that particular box to begin with. Those almost-always-plastic freebies were packed by a machine with a diabolical commitment to delayed gratification, so that the prize was invariably positioned in the most inaccessible place in the box.

My parents had a no-hands-in-the-box-digging-for-the-prize policy. The rule was that the kid who *incidentally* came across the prize when pouring cereal out got to keep it. This made for eager anticipation and sharp competition with my sisters, as well as some extra-large bowls of cereal (is that smart marketing or what?). A kid who was bold enough to use the hand-in-the-box technique when no one was looking had to wait until its content went down some, anyway, in order to insert both hand *and* forearm into the box to fish around for that buried treasure. Otherwise, like Archimedes with his bath, he or she would discover the principle that the volume of cereal equal to that of the inserted appendage would end up spilled on the table or floor. I don't know this from personal experience, of course.

Less immediate, but maybe more intensely fun, were the really cool things a kid could send away for. Sometimes these were free, if the official order blank was accompanied by several box tops ("Mom, can't we buy *three* boxes, so I don't have to wait?"). Other times they cost fifty cents or a dollar—plus the box tops. Either way, the anticipation was stretched out, if not heightened, by the invariable "'Allow six to eight weeks for delivery." Even the Pony Express didn't take that long, so I'm guessing that in an era when "Made in Japan" was synonymous with "cheap," delivery came from halfway around the world. At any rate, getting something in the mail, addressed *to me*, was a rare and special pleasure in itself.

Maybe the best of the few things my folks let me send away for was a "submarine" that was a plastic tube about a quarter inch in diameter and a couple inches long, with a bubble on top in the middle. It had a plug in one end that could be pulled to add a small amount of baking soda. This made the sub dive and surface repeatedly when put into a pan of water or the bathtub. I had a lot of fun with that, for at least a day or two.

***

The vast majority of my childhood, outside of school, was spent playing down at the lake, out in the woods, at the sledding hill, or on my bike. Since I grew up in an area with immediate access to woods and water, my spending a good deal of time outside might not have been typical for all kids then. I did, however, have at least some insight into how city kids lived from visiting my own cousins "in town," and it wasn't all that different. There were tradeoffs, but the real action was still outside.

Two or three times a year, we'd pack up the car for the six-hour or so drive to Ohio. A few times, when my dad couldn't get away from work, my mom and sisters and I took the train from Detroit to Dayton. I was very young, so cruelly, since I *loved* trains, all that I can say I truly remember was the vastness of the railroad station and the peculiar smell of the rail car, which for some reason I relate to the inside of a Chinese restaurant. Once, I even took the bus by myself. This experience is immortalized by getting my wallet stolen, I am certain, by the guy sitting next to me. I had saved up seven dollars to spend in my week staying with my cousins, and I was devastated, but once again wiser in the ways of the world.

Once arrived in Miamisburg, what was cool about being in town was that there were so many interesting things I could walk to, with many more things of interest along the way. Although they were different things from home, the process of discovery was similar, except here there were sidewalks. There were also raised curbs along some of them that I loved to see how long I could walk on without losing my balance. I wonder how many gymnasts started off this way?

About three blocks away and halfway between my grandparents' houses, there was a neighborhood drug store with a soda fountain. Stopping here, en route, for an ice cream cone was a darn good excuse for walking from one grandparent's house to the other. Even though we only came to town a few times a year, the proprietor quickly got to know me by name and who I was related to. Across the street from the drug store was the city park with a water fountain and a band shell. A couple of times we were fortunate enough to hear an actual band concert here.

One of my grandmas, who was chubby and jolly and chuckled a lot, worked at a bakery, four or five blocks the other way, toward downtown. We kids would either walk to the bakery to visit her and get a treat, or she'd bring one home for us. It usually would be cream horns that were way too high and wide with flakey pastry to even imagine getting our mouth around, or a German crumb-top coffee cake. These were special treats, because there either wasn't a real bakery close to us at home, or my parents didn't patronize one. Our bakery was the A&P. Fortunately, my mother knew the secret of the Miamisburg bakery coffee cakes and would make one for us once in a while.

Downtown Miamisburg was another several blocks further. It had a large drugstore, Philhower's, a five and dime, and its own movie theater. If we were lucky, we kids got to take in a Saturday matinee at the theater during our visits. I'm not sure if this always fell under the heading of "fun," however. One movie we saw, *The Creature Walks Among Us*, scared the heck out of me and made me very leery for some time about walking up the shadowy stairs to the upstairs bedrooms in my paternal grandparents' old house.

We usually stayed with my dad's parents, whose small city yard was always lined with flowers and had a tiny vegetable plot in one back corner, bordering the alley. Southern Ohio was several weeks ahead of us in the growing season, and if it were Easter time, the Easter lilies would be blooming. I would love to go out into the back yard and stick my nose into them to inhale their incomparable fragrance—and get a yellow nose from the pollen. They will always be part of the smell of spring for me.

If it were a bit later in the year, I could snitch a few strawberries from the ones my grandpa always put out. I wish I could get some plants, now, of the variety he planted, then. They were the tastiest non-wild strawberries ever. My other granddad grew roses and put out several tomato plants every year. After losing his farm, I don't think he had the heart to grow anything else, but he was always extremely proud of his regal roses and killer tomatoes. The roses I liked, but the tomatoes didn't impress me, since I couldn't tolerate the taste of raw tomatoes.

Once when I was quite young, we were down at the time cherries were ripe. My Aunt Mildred, Uncle Ray, and their kids lived a few doors down from my dad's parent's then, in a house with a broadly spreading sour cherry tree in the back yard. I can remember sitting up in that tree with my cousin Ronnie eating our fill and then some of cherries. My grandmother would can these cherries, peaches from the small tree in her own back yard, and wild blackberries. The peach tree was as slight as the cherry tree was hefty. My grandfather had planted it from a peach pit way back when, so it was a true heritage variety of some sort. Getting back to its roots obviously was a good thing; it was a prolific producer and its peaches had that good old-time taste, just like the strawberries.

The blackberries came from summer Saturdays at the Germantown dam. Blackberry picking was and still is a family tradition. According to my father, my grandpa would take him, his brothers and every possible container they could find, and they'd go out and pick "twenty gallons" of blackberries. Not, however, before they had rubbed themselves with Lifeboy soap to repel the chiggers. When we'd visit in my own childhood, there were always rows of quart jars of canned fruit on the shelves in my grandparents' root cellar. This included blackberries, so my grandfather had continued his picking long after his kids had left home and acquired little pickers of their own.

The root cellar, complete with dead air, cobwebs and a dirt floor, was accessed by skeletal wood steps under double doors that pulled up from the side-porch floor, opposite the porch swing. It was the closest I'd ever come to being in a mine, but it didn't take much work to come up with some jewel-like Mason jars of the canned fruit that were staples for desserts at Grandma's house. Unfortunately, the cherries ended before long, when the cherry tree and its house were torn down to make way for a new school building.

Just the other side of and behind the house with the cherry tree was the school yard and playground for the Catholic school. Before they demolished the old three-story school to make way for the new, my cousins, sisters, and I would act out all kinds of fantastic games, playing on the three-floor fire escapes for the school, which came all the way down to the ground and provided easy access. We'd also play on the swings and slide, which we transformed to super-slick by sitting on waxed paper as we slid down. The playground equipment was for me, however, just a pastime while waiting for the trains.

The double track of the New York Central ran directly behind the playground, and I'd listen for the hum of the rails and the anticipatory whistle far up the track. At last the flickering head light would show, and everything would revert to slow motion. Like a watched tea kettle getting ready to boil, the light would ever so slowly steady into the Cyclops eye in the round black face of the chuffing magnificent monster that emerged in a cacophony of hissing and squeal of wheels. Then, we could see the engineer on his high throne pull the cord to whistle a warning for the crossing ahead. Usually, his window would be open and he'd wave to his little fan club. After the crazy, heartbeat cadence of car-space, car-space, car-space, there often would be a conductor in the caboose to wave goodbye and convince me, once again, that this roaring, clackety-clacking monster had a good heart.

Occasionally a train would stop right behind the schoolyard, and a few times I got to talk with an engineer. Because I was totally in love with trains, every train that went by was a great treat for me. I would count the cars on every one, trying to find the ultimately long train. When diesel engines started being mixed in with the steam locomotives, I found them fascinating, because they were new. I couldn't wait to see the next one slip into the queue of suddenly stodgy-seeming steam locomotives. Then, the friendly coal-black, fire-breathing monsters were gone. Little did I know how much I would miss them.

I was aware pretty early on of the irony of people having gardens and fruit trees in their yards in the city, especially since my family didn't have either in the country. I saw the other advantages of city living, too. Miamisburg had a baseball/softball park, complete with concession stand, with games every night under the lights; a large municipal swimming pool with a high dive; restaurants and the movie theater you could walk to. My cousins walked to school. My own neighborhood did have counterparts to or compensations for most of the city amenities. Some, the lake for instance, were better; some, like the movies and restaurants were farther away and required parents and cars to take advantage of. Having a train going by regularly, right in your back yard, however, was almost a complete wipeout for my home turf. There were two lines that ran a few miles away from me in opposite directions. On a quiet night, with my bedroom window open, I could hear their mournful whistles calling in the distance, and I'd wonder where the lucky people on them were going. It was romantic and it was mesmerizing, but it was also like having the squeal of the pig, instead of the ham and the bacon.

***

When I got my own bedroom, the opening to the attic was in my ceiling. Standing on a six-foot ladder from the garage, I could push out the light board that fit into the opening and climb into the attic. Once up, I pulled the string on the naked bulb overhead and began discovering that my parents had a history. It may not have been an exceptional history, but the fact that they had a life prior to us kids was intriguing. My seven or eight year-old self took my parents as a matter of fact. I knew the outline of their background, but here were artifacts, suggestions that there were real people behind the mom and dad role players.

My dad had been in the service in World War II, something I vaguely knew, but here I found, among the clothes hanging on a wire strung from the rafters, beautiful silk kimonos he had bought in Japan after the war and brought home for my mother. I also found a couple of bayonets he had gotten during the war, a German one and an Italian one. I discovered a tin box that used to house a first-aid kit, full of foreign currency and coins, as well as an envelope of loose pearls and cameos. Wow! This was the source of a whole bunch of questions I would otherwise never have known to ask.

My dad was in the Merchant Marine during World War II and didn't talk much about it. This may well have been the result of the "brush off" treatment Merchant Marine sailors got after the war. Despite the fact that the Merchant Marines suffered by far the greatest percentage killed of any of the services and were absolutely critical to the war effort, they received no benefits after the war, and not even so much as a thank you. My dad had artifacts from both the European and Asian war theaters from the multiple trips he made on Liberty Ships to both. It has only been recently that I discovered the true role of the Merchant Marine in the war. At the same time I found a small snapshot of my dad and some of his bearded sailing buddies on board ship. I had this enlarged and restored and presented it to him along with a book recounting the first-person experiences of many Merchant Mariners during the war. His tears of joy prove that even tears can be fun.

Answering a lot of questions, but raising even more, were my parents' high school yearbooks. There were pictures of my mother, the drum majorette, leading the band and flinging her baton into the air. There were also newspaper clips about her and her younger brother, my other Uncle John, who was a football star. These were in a cardboard box half full with a big pile of loose photographs, some of them going back to my parents' childhood or farther. What a trip to see my parents for the first time as children themselves and as teenagers!

Maybe the biggest surprise was that these pictures even existed. My parents weren't big on taking photos. I think we had one box camera (it took 620 film, as I recall), but I don't specifically remember them taking snapshots, and there are not that many pictures of *any* of us before this time that weren't professionally taken. We got better after this, and the number of pictures eventually multiplied. I got my own Brownie camera at some point, but I followed my family tradition and didn't take many pictures until I had children of my own. Part of the reason for all this is that film was always expensive and developing even more so. I also think my parents' generation wasn't so self-absorbed that they thought very much of their lives was important enough to record for posterity—or for them to look at a week later. It has been great for me, however, to look at these family pictures, and though I wish there were more of them, their scarcity contributes to their value.

***

One of my biggest attic finds was a couple of boxes of old books. These also gave me some pretty good insight into who my parents were, even though I didn't realize it at the time. I think you can tell a lot about a person by what he or she reads, and even more by what books he or she saves. The most immediately interesting to me of my dad's old books was *The River Motor Boat Boys On the Amazon*. It was the first in an eight-book series by Harry Gordon, from 1913. Six daring teenage boys in three boats plied the Amazon, and later seven other rivers, saving the world from some really bad guys. It was the first young adult chapter book I had ever attempted, and though it took a while, I was very proud of myself when I finished it.

Reading became for me a pleasure and an adventure. I read every book I could that interested me in my pretty limited school library. There were strict limitations on what books what grades could read, so it didn't take long to go through them. Fortunately, about the same time, I discovered the branch of the public library that was only a couple of miles from me, as the crow flies. It was across the neighborhood that was on the other side of the woods from me. At this point in my young life, it was like another country, especially since it was even in another school district. The library was in the upstairs of the large barn-like structure that was the club house for this neighborhood. My older sister and I were taking accordion lessons, and the instructor had periodic recitals for his students at this club house. It was before or after one of these recitals that I made the exciting discovery of the library upstairs. It was then simply a matter of figuring out how to get there on foot or bicycle. Fortunately, the shortcut through the woods was only about one-third the distance by car.

Going to the library and reading became essential parts of my life. For some reason, my preferred position for reading was lying on my side with my head propped up by one forearm, and my cheek in the palm of my hand. When I'd turn a page, I would switch sides. I remember adopting this posture in the grass in my front yard, on the living room floor, and on my bed, but I don't specifically recall *sitting* and reading a book, except in school. Maybe this was because I didn't read for fun in school—except when I'd put my library book under my school book and read it on the sly.

***

We always had a TV I don't remember the first 8" one. I do remember the coming of the new 19" one; it was a beauty—beige Masonite-like case perched on a black, wrought iron stand. The black and white picture was as life-like as…a newspaper. We were fortunate enough to get four channels. All three American networks were there, and, since we were close to Windsor, Ontario, we got Canadian TV too. This was an especial advantage, because I got to learn about Esso gasoline and Molson Canadian beer early on, since these were the sponsors of *Hockey Night In Canada,*" on Saturday nights during hockey season. "He shoots…he scoooooores!" and "a *great save* by Sawchuck!" became part of the common language of my buddy Denny and me when he got a table-top hockey game for Christmas. We played incessantly for a few months, until I figured out that I could almost never beat him.

Because there were so many other things to do, TV watching was quite deliberate. You didn't just turn the TV on; you turned it on to watch something in particular. There were definitely some things that attracted my attention and loyalty. A very early one was *Lunch With Soupy.* This noon-time comedic extravaganza headed by the inimitable Soupy Sales was *my* Sesame Street. He was the only human on stage, but his cast included Willy the Worm, "the sickest worm in *all* of Detroit", who lived in a miniature trailer on his table, and arms and voices only of White Fang, "the meanest dog in *all* Detroit" and Black Tooth, "the sweetest dog in *all* Detroit." There were also hand puppets in the window of Soupy's lunch room: Pooky the Lion, who would sing things like "Catch a pickled herring/put it in a barrel/Save it for a rainy day," to the tune of "Catch a Falling Star," and Hippy the Hippo. Both would act as foils for Soupy or he for them—showcasing Soupy's talent to do both. I would be very surprised if these routines didn't inspire Jim Henson with his Muppets.

Then, there was the guy with the gruff voice, who would knock on the back door. Soupy would do a double-take and answer it. You'd never see this guy but he'd always start off "Mr. Sales?" as if he were there to deliver something. A short goofy conversation would ensue and it would inevitably end up with the guy delivering a pie to Soupy's face. Next to the door was a plug in the wall with a "Do Not Touch" sign under it. Periodically, and as if he'd never seen the thing before, Soupy would notice the plug, kind of look around to see if anyone was watching, pull the plug and look in the hole. His curiosity often got him a stream of water in the face, but he never learned.

Lunch With Soupy was nominally a kid's show, but Soupy's material was very sophisticated and his delivery was so masterful that it would keep my mother in stitches. It also was live, and no tapes were made of the show. That's an entertainment tragedy, because the fun we lucky few had having lunch with Soupy will be gone forever when we are.

A later show I loved so much that I'd usually come home from anything else I was doing to watch, was the *Mickey Mouse Club*. Love is a strong motivator, and I was head over heels for Annette (okay, what male kid then wasn't?). It was Annette and all of the Mousketeers who were the draw. They were talented kids, but they were presented as kids next door. They were actually *better* than this, because they were always super nice and unassuming. Most of all, these kids, with whom we all could identify, were living a perfect life that any of us would have given anything to be part of. Add to this some extremely appealing (for the same reasons) serials, such as *Spin and Marty* and *The Hardy Boys*, and we couldn't wait to see what each new day would bring. At the end of the show, all of the Mousketeers would sing: "M-I-C," and Jimmy Dodd would say "*See* you real soon," "K-E-Y," "*Why*, because we *like* you." "M-O-U-S-E." I'm sure not many kids in TV land, if they thought about it, considered that all those great Mousketeers *really did* like them, but I'll bet almost every one of us believed it.

Another show, that my whole family had a date for, was *Maverick*. This was on Sunday night, and the tradition we established was that my mother would make Chef Boyarde pizzas and we would all sit, eating pizza, watching Maverick outsmart the bad guys. As a professional Wild West gambler, the title character, played to perfection by James Garner, was an allegory. In a sleazy profession, he was meticulously honest, and he always won in the end, because he was good at heart and because he was smart. The seemingly ultimate pragmatist who would rather run than fight, he consistently proved himself to be principled and brave, usually in spite of his best intentions. It was all done with a great and pleasing sense of humor.

One of my very favorite shows was *Have Gun Will Travel*. It was on Saturdays, just before *Gunsmoke*. (What a glorious doubleheader of serious westerns!) Surprisingly there wasn't a whole lot of discussion about whether *Have Gun* was appropriate for kids. It was, after all, about a sophisticated and educated man, who would periodically leave San Francisco culture to track people down and bring them to justice—dead or alive. It also was one of the most philosophical shows ever on TV There was much more than the today's template of good versus evil laid over some gratuitous violence or perversion. When Paladin accepted a job and switched into his all-black jeans, shirt, and boots, it was never without thoughtful consideration of ethics and compassionate consideration of the human beings involved. Some of the time, he would decide *not* to bring back a fugitive, whom he decided didn't deserve to be punished. Like *Maverick*, *Have Gun Will Travel* broke through the law of the Western jungle and the wimpy rationale of "He drew first." This show started me thinking, at an early age about the why's of right and wrong, and, I am sure, influenced my decision to major in philosophy in college.

When my own children were growing up, TV played a limited role by design. They did watch the very first Sesame Street episode at ages two and a half and one, respectively, and continued to watch the show regularly. (Because I was reviewing it for a newspaper, my daughters even got to sit on the original Miss Susan's lap and chat with her after a *Sesame Street Live* performance—fun for me *and* them). Instead, we went to lots of live music and other performances. Since we always lived around universities, it was easy to find inexpensive or free performances. My wife and I also read to our children regularly. We were able to share many really great books with them, some of which were beyond their ability to read themselves, along with commentary and explanation by Mom and Dad. This helped them to learn life-important lessons at an early age, while enjoying great literature.

As for the TV in our lives, therein lies a story that's near and dear to my family. You've heard the expression "Kill your TV"? I did it. One day my wife was away and I was watching the kids. I had delegated the job of watching their one and a half year-old brother to my two daughters, while I went down to the garage to do something or other. When I came back a short time later, *he* had climbed up onto the kitchen counter and was helping himself Winnie the Pooh style to a five pound jar of honey. *They* had their eyes glued to the TV about fifteen feet away. I called their attention to the situation, walked over, and (calmly, I swear) picked up the

TV, carried it to the close-by front door, and bounced it off the cement front porch that ran the length of the house. It felt remarkably good, and I left it there. While my daughters sat in stunned silence (great way to get attention), I cleaned up my sticky little Pooh-boy.

There were no more arguments over how much TV anyone would watch. We didn't have a TV for four years, until we inherited one from my younger sister, when she died in a car accident. I am absolutely sure we all were better for it.

We're gonna rock, gonna rock,
around the clock tonight

Jerry Lee Lewis

Chapter Sixteen

Fun, Fun, Fun

I could never beat my little sister at cards, well, hardly ever. She was three years younger, and she had uncanny card sense. We'd mostly play casino or double solitaire, and she would delight in taking down her big bro. My whole family were card players. My mother belonged to a neighborhood canasta club when I was little (bunco, too). She and my dad also belonged to several pinochle clubs over the years, and they would often go out on Saturday night to play cards with friends.

On the Friday or Saturday nights they didn't go out, my mom would pop a big bowl of popcorn, and our whole family would play rummy or pinochle, cribbage or euchre. I have always had a hard time understanding why some "moralists" are so against card playing. Not only is it a powerful educational tool—learning and applying the rules, developing strategy, math, logic—it's great way to develop social skills. From competition to cooperating with a partner; to bluffing and bantering; to learning to be a good sport, win or lose, cards mirror the real game of life.

Maybe it's gambling at cards that some find sinful. I unabashedly admit to often, as a kid, playing cards for money with my family. That just made everything more fun. My dad kept a two-pound coffee can filled with pennies, nickels, and dimes to act as the bank. Early on, he would stake us kids, but it was much better to play with our own dollar or two.

119

Then he would say, "That's not going to last long!" Sometimes it did, and sometimes it didn't. If we lost, we didn't get our money back; this was real. Admittedly, winning and losing didn't feel the same. Either way, it wasn't much, and the idea was that even if you lost, the fun you had was worth the price of admission.

When we'd have extended family gatherings, the cards would often come out at night for the many variations of poker. It was a way for kids and adults to interact as equals and for kids to learn some important qualities of being an adult. We learned the skills and the realities of gambling at an early age, everything from keeping a poker face to "Never bet more than you can afford to lose." My favorite lesson, passed on from my grandpa through my dad, is: "When you win a pot, put half of it into your pocket to keep, and play only with the other half." When we grew up, none of us had a problem with overdoing gambling. We were savvy to the reality of it; besides, to us it was still a family thing.

We played many other games—we kids among ourselves and as a family—everything from Candy Land to Scrabble, checkers and chess, Chinese checkers and a similar game called Yahoo, dominoes, Yahtzee, Clue, and the Game of Life. Heck, this *was* life, or at the very least, it was really living.

***

In addition to the natural world of play outside—sledding, swimming, building forts, plus reading, TV and games, there was the almost superfluous element of toys. I know, a toy can be almost anything, and almost anything can be turned into a toy. But, I'm talking about the things, mostly bought from the store, that were designated as toys, the kind of thing we got for birthdays or at Christmas. Neither of these occasions resulted in big hauls for the kids in my family. My parents definitely didn't have a lot of money to spend, and credit cards were not yet a common exchange medium. Curiously, the lack of credit actually meant people had more money to spend in the end. Since, with the exception of mortgages and cars, they only bought what they could pay cash for or they put larger items in layaway and paid a little at a time, people didn't spend anything on interest or service charges. The same was true for merchants, who didn't have to pay a percentage of sales to a credit card company.

For Christmas, we'd get one "big" present, generally a toy, and most of the rest would be clothes or something else we needed. Our "bigs" were not usually the biggest or best of their types, but we learned to be satisfied with what we got, and I think we also learned that toys just aren't that important. Some of the presents I especially remember start with one of those deluxe filling station and garages, with a ramp that circles up to the top. "Driving" my little cars into that thing was a source of never-ending amusement to me.

Another vehicular favorite was a big yellow earth mover, with doors in its belly that opened to let out its load of dirt. Since my favorite medium for play was in the dirt, this was a perfect toy. Also in this category was an electric train. It was a basic set up with enough track to make up only about a 2 1/2 x 4 foot oval. Since the house was so small, I couldn't leave even that set up for long. Given my love of trains, this was not quite the thrill it might have been. The fact that my pal Denny had a bigger, more deluxe train package permanently set up on his back porch contributed to my disappointment.

Later on, the things that stand out are a chemistry set, a microscope, and a telescope. None of these were the top of the line, which, like the train, limited their usefulness. They *were* the best my parents could do, but it was hard sometimes to feel good about this. It was a lot easier to notice the kids who got more than I did rather than those who got less. I think I actually felt worse for my parents, though, than I did for myself. The toys truly weren't that important. What I understood, early on, was important was letting my parents know I thought they were the best parents in the world.

This was equally difficult, if not harder, when it came to gift giving. When we were first old enough to buy presents, my dad would supplement what little we might have been able to save with maybe five or ten dollars. I remember blowing almost my whole stake one year on some Channel No. 5 cologne for my mother. I'm not sure if she ever actually used it, but it made me happy to buy it for her, and I'm sure that made *her* happy. Other years, I remember buying her a small bronzed glass powder holder with a fawn on top of the cover, a fancy rose and clear glass pedestal candy dish, and a red glass pitcher and glass set. I know these were good choices because she used and displayed them and had still them when she died. I have them now, reminders of Christmas love.

***

Winter was a kid's wonderland in Oakland County, Michigan, but summer was just plain wonderful. Summer days were sun-baked pleasure of woods and water, and summer nights were the icing on top. A plain vanilla night might involve going out into a steamy backyard with a flashlight after a rain to pinch night crawlers to prevent them from retracting, like steel tapes, into their holes. This, in the vain hope that bigger worms might catch bigger fish. On a drier, less worm-friendly night, we might turn the flashlight away from the ground to a game of flashlight tag. This was one of several night games we'd play with vision like owls, sharpened from an early age by stretching the meaning of "dark," when we were supposed to be in by dark.

Other nights we'd hunker down around a fire for some round-robin, mostly scary story telling. There was a primordial fascination in flickering flames. The heat and light seemed energize the storyteller in us and bring out stories we didn't know we knew. This mystical camaraderie would be periodically interrupted by a shift in the night breeze and the smoke. This would cause a scramble for new positions to avoid stinging eyes and asphyxiation. Talk about second-hand smoke!

These sessions were always in the yard of brothers Jim and Charlie. Ironically, Jim became a smoke jumper and world traveler, Charlie a talented wood carver and furniture maker. Those sessions also left the smell of smoke deeply engrained in my character. The best way to describe this might be through the poem I wrote years later on my way to one of the many open-mike poetry readings I used to participate in in Ann Arbor.

Into the Light

Poets, hunkering down for solitude,
gather singly before the smoldering fire
to poke sticks, charred to a point,
into coals to make flame.
Shadows flicker, heat rises,
and the poets risk getting burned
by a tenacious spark,
getting too warm on one side,
cold on the other,
smelling of smoke for days.
Still, it's more than moths
that fly into the light,
unable to resist their nature.

Another way that campfires entered into summer nights was when my across-the-street pal, Jim, and I would camp out in a clearing in the little woods across the street the other way from his house. On either side of our small campfire, we'd spread out our bedrolls, just like in the TV westerns. Jim, in fact, had moved into the neighborhood from Tucson, and was a self-styled expert on how to make up a camp bed. It was extremely important, he insisted, that we tuck our upper blankets firmly underneath the ones on the ground to keep out scorpions. Even though this was scorpion-free Michigan, his advice seemed sound, since there were various other critters you didn't want to sleep with.

We would gradually drift off into sleep rendered tenuous by wild night sounds as loud as if someone had left both the TV and the radio on. This night concert was a treasure akin to the wild berries I loved to gather. It was even better, more transparent and distinct, than what I heard through my open bedroom window every night. There were visuals, too. Light pollution was low, and the night sky, with its chiaroscuro interplay of clouds, moon, and stars, was always fascinating. This was especially so to a kid, at the edge of the space era, who loved science fiction.

Lying on the ground, itself, wasn't exactly a sleep aid, as the topography of the ground didn't take long to make a negative impression upon my back. Then, the chill of the Michigan night would begin to penetrate my albeit scorpion-proof, blanket. On one magical moonless night, I was awake and looking up at just the right times to see the just- launched Echo satellite winking at me as it passed over seven times. I know this is true, since I have told the story so many times. Alternatively, if it isn't true, I've told it so many times it ought to be.

***

Years later, when I or one of my friends would have access to a car, our summer night odysseys would go well beyond the neighborhood in search of something cool to do. This would sometimes involve the period classic of cruisin'. The real deal would involve driving fifteen miles of so over to suburban Detroit's Woodward Ave. The place to be on our end of Woodward was Ted's, a high-toned drive-in on the edge of Pontiac but actually in Bloomfield Township, one of the wealthiest in the country. It was no pick-up place for us kids from considerably less well-to-do neighborhoods, but it was a great place to indulge our imaginations. The real action, though, was out on the boulevard, where a fast car was the socio-economic equalizer, and the really hot cars and a host of wannabes would see who could beat whom off the line at the turn of the light, and still avoid the cops.

The food was great at Ted's, but a bit pricey. If it was simply stomach hunger that we needed to assuage, next door Pontiac was the place. It had the only McDonald's around, and the only one I knew of anywhere for a long time. In high school, my friends and I generally went to the Red Barn, on the closer side of town, for our 15¢ hamburgers and fries. It was still two burgers, fries, and a shake, with change from our dollar.

Some of the other things we did on summer nights, I don't care to mention. I'd just as soon that the generation in my family on either side of me remains blissfully ignorant. I take my cue from my own kids, who were "model teenagers," but who tell me that I wouldn't want to know some of the things *they* did. They're right, I don't.

Regardless of what adventure transpired earlier, summer nights ended up the same. This usually meant thinking about what *could* have been. On hot nights it also meant tossin' and turnin' in a bedroom that was way hotter than any of the night's action. For all of my childhood, my family did not possess an air conditioner, nor did they much believe in fans. It was open windows all the way, hence my considerable familiarity with night sounds. My bedroom had a casement window, about four feet by three feet, that opened inward and was propped open with a piece of wood. Relief from the heat for a body usually still radiating from a day at The Beach, meant turning rotisserie style onto a new, cool spot on the sheet

***

As I write this, I just saw what I think is a highly unusual thing. There was an ad in the local weekly newspaper for "Teen Dances" in the big room at a local restaurant that usually is the venue for buffets and concerts by area country music bands. Being out of the market, I may be woefully uninformed about such things, but this is the first teen dance outside of a school gym I've seen in a long, long time. When I was dancin' age, there were so many dances going on in various communities that usually kids had a choice of which one they wanted to go to. Of course, until I or one of my friends turned sixteen and got the family wheels for the night, I went to the place that was easiest to get to, that is, that my parents would take me to.

There were dances at churches and community centers, and there were even some private businesses that sponsored them. In the summer, these included dances in the sand at different beaches. The closest dances for me were at our very own neighborhood club house. This was an old barn-like structure that once was part of a country club. A community group had gotten together and sold shares to buy it for $10,000. Then, members or anyone who cared to was asked to provide the labor to refurbish the building. The inside was in pretty good shape, but the outside required many, many hours and gallons of paint to put it back into decent shape. My dad, the paint contractor, of course was in charge of the painting and spent untold hours working on the building.

When it was done, the Club House was a wonderful community asset. We had potluck dinners there frequently, often in association with work bees. I got a chance to see what other kids in the neighborhood were eating and compare it to my mom's cooking. There was a pool table downstairs and an upright piano on the main floor, just right for plinking out "Heart and Soul." In the summer, I shot in a kids' archery league on the front lawn.

More than anything, however, the main floor was a huge open space, perfect for weddings, parties, and dances. These were either money-making rentals, or Community Association sponsored activities for adults. After a while, however, and just in time for me, periodic teen dances were put on by the Association, and then weekly summer dances. This was the hottest spot around, first, because there was no air conditioning. All those wildly gyrating bodies created a tremendous amount of heat, which made regular trips out to the veranda across the front and the cool night air a necessity. Kids came and went, including to the cars that were parked on the front lawn, and there was never a problem.

Another way these dances were hot is that there was always live music from rockin' local bands, of which there was no shortage. The hottest thing, though, was that this was the place to be. It was located near the line of two school districts and drew heavily from both. This gave kids a chance to meet and get down with a whole new crop of potential boyfriends and girlfriends. That was pretty much the goal of all the guys I knew. The girls, on the other hand, seemed to lean more towards just loving to dance.

These dances were something for us kids to really look forward to, something designed just for us, that let us do all the things that we really loved doing. There seemed to be no hidden agenda by the adults who sponsored them, and I believe that just about every kid who had half a thought in his or her head realized that this was a good thing and appreciated it. Consequently, we very typical teenagers were on our best behavior. Everyone had a lot of fun, and it was great exercise, too.

***

There weren't dances every night of the week in the summer, so what did we teenagers do on other nights? The venue of choice was the drive in. I suppose I should qualify this with "movie," since for a lot of kids "drive in" might also refer to a restaurant where you sat in the car and ordered food through a speaker. Wasn't modern technology great? A *really* high-tech date might include both a drive-in movie *and* food at a drive-in restaurant. The restaurants we always called by name. You went to the Big Boy, or to A&W, or to Ted's. On the other hand, if we were going to a movie, it was just to going to the drive-in.

Drive-ins were a terrible deterrent to teenage boys' watching movies. The combination of peer expectations and those fabled hormones, made the movie only a background for the real reason for being there. That was, of course, to see "how far you could go" with your date. The possibilities for this only began if your date was sitting close to you; it didn't count if you had to move over close to her. It she wasn't sitting close, your relationship was defined as "only friends," the rest of the program was forestalled, and you might as well watch the movie. Even in this pitiable case, the movie might be hard to focus on, as the guy's mind was working hard to figure out a way to get his date to sit closer.

Assuming that his date was sitting fairly close, a guy could proceed to put on the moves. The first might be to lean his right knee over, ever so slowly, until it is touching hers. Obviously, if the distance is too great, the subtlety of the move is lost to a long and unlovely leg stretch. With initial contact made, the next move is to get that right arm, which is looming on the seat back, to drop inch by inch until it makes contact with a female shoulder. It's important to not take too long to accomplish this. Maintaining the "arm overhang" position for extended periods can cause the blood to drain from the arm, numbness, shoulder pain, and other unpleasant symptoms. (This is the voice of experience speaking.) Once arm/shoulder touch is established, the guys hand becomes a marvelous tool and messenger of love. It can close over her shoulder and pull her closer, caress her upper arm, and...well, you know.

I first heard the term "passion pit" used to refer to drive-ins by my Aunt Mildred. Since it was well before my capacity for "passion" had developed, I assume that the previous generation did more than watch the movie when they went to drive-ins. I know that for my generation, some serious making out went on in cars while the movies played on. A lot more was learned about biology, or at least anatomy, in the back seat than in the high school lab. I personally never heard of anyone going "all the way" at the drive-in, but I do know that everything else was alleged to happen and happen frequently.

Disregard by some teenagers of the actual movie being shown at the drive-in may have had its genesis in visits as little kids, with their parents.

Because the movie couldn't be shown until it got dark, it was often bedtime for us younguns before the movie was well under way. Of course by that time we had already spent half an hour playing on the playground that most drive-ins provided, increasing our tendency to nod off. Back in the car, we'd help roll up the windows when the truck came around spraying a dense fog of mosquito killer (DDT?). After we steamed in the windows-up heat (there was no air conditioning) while the fog settled, we'd crank 'em down and get ready for the cartoons, which you could never see that well, since it was still too light. Then it was time for us kids to start begging for my parents to break out the popcorn my mother always popped and the Kool Aid. Everything to this point, along with getting to sleep in the car, was sufficient fun in itself for us, as little kids, at the drive-in.

Whatever drinks my parents would bring for us set off the inevitable need to visit the concession stand and the bathrooms.

The movie, during which I will always remember falling asleep, is *The Bible* (at least I think that's the title; I can't find it anywhere). I remember it's being very dramatic; the Noah's ark scene is emblazoned in my mind forever. The water was rising right up to the top of the highest hill. Women were clinging to rocks with one hand and holding up babies in the other, desperately looking up to the heavens. It really freaked me out, especially after the indiscriminate destruction of Sodom and Gomorrah, and I wondered how in the world God could do such a thing to the innocent people along with the guilty. Then I fell asleep. Just as well, I guess; the *Bible* is full of lessons that I'm afraid are R-rated, even if they are only believable to child-like minds.

***

Now, let's suppose that you're a guy and you have access to a car, but no date. There were still endless things you could do with some of your pals. There was Putt-Putt (aka miniature golf). This was a bit like video games now, or pinball then, insofar as to get good at it you would have to practice multiple times, which could get expensive. It had the advantage, though, of being an equally fun place to go with "the guys" (for the competition) or to take a date. For a while, there were also a number of trampoline places, where you could pay for a half-hour of time on the tramp. These were set at ground level, and the mats were smaller than full size tramps. There was a padded buffer around the outside, but it wasn't very wide. Beyond that was--you guessed it--concrete, and then another tramp. Gee, I wonder what the liability was on those things, and I wonder why they didn't last long. Another possibility for fun and law suits, that I haven't seen around for awhile, is the go-kart track. I guess it went the way of the rent-a-motorcycle place.

Small Japanese motorcycles, with 50-125 c.c. engines, enjoyed a surge in popularity in the 60's. Of course, not many of us kids could afford to buy one for $300 or so, but we could afford to rent one by the hour, so cycle rental places sprung up to meet the market. There was even one for short while in Walled Lake, the small town close to where I lived.

The appeal to teens was immense: a motorized vehicle we could go fast on and *feel* it, plus Honda's irresistible slogan "You meet the nicest people on a Honda." Of course, we guys were hoping some of those people would be attractive females. That couldn't have been much on our minds the day a bunch of us Walled Lake High guys skipped school and rented motorcycles (seems like Yamaha 90's). The girls were all back in school, but we had a great time anyway. We even managed not to hurt ourselves, though I did some damage to my pants when I wiped out trying to turn too sharply.

***

Many of the things we did for fun as kids were much more physically dangerous, because they were real, than things kids do today on screens. Although we may have occasionally done more damage to skin or bones, what we did in the sun, in trees, on bikes, was also far less violent than much of what kids now do virtually. One of Nature's purposes for youthful fun is to let kids try new things and learn through the consequences for doing the wrong things. A skinned knee or a bump on the head was a good learning tool for us, though admittedly some of us were slow learners. I fear that kids today, overprotected from sun and scrapes, may end up, in the long run, suffering far greater consequences than they would have from the bumps and bruises of real life fun.

CHAPTER SEVENTEEN

Music

There were many opportunities to experience first-rate popular musical performances up close and personal in the days before the economy of size dictated bigger and less personal venues. There still was an admission charge, though, so a steady diet was out of the question for me. Instead, my live music experience came most of the time right next door. My buddy Jim was musical and played drums and guitar. He was frequently involved in some sort of rock band, which often practiced at his house It was interesting and easy enough to follow the progress of Jim's band—even when I was *next door,* at my house.

Better, was where Jim got his musical sense from. His dad played guitar and also was part of a band. This band was pretty constant in its personnel, and was darned good. They played country and western music, both traditional and popular, and played mostly for the fun of it. They also practiced, some of the time, at Jim's house, and it was no problem to go over and listen to them make music. By "make music," I mean that I could watch and hear what went into getting a song just the way they wanted it. Since these guys played together all the time, it wasn't all starts and stops, either. There was a lot of jamming and a lot of joy. They loved making music, and I loved listening to them make it.

Being so appreciative of and fascinated by o.p.m. (other people's music), I can't say why the bug to play myself never bit me. My older sister and I did take accordion lessons for a while. Why accordion, I don't know; my folks didn't even watch Lawrence Welk! But, there were way too many other things to do, and though I loved music, I didn't necessarily love the accordion or practicing it. Summer beckoned, and it was during the summer that my parents let both of us quit.

Another source of good live music experience was school, notably in the form of band, vocal, and orchestral concerts and the spring musical. For me, this didn't happen until high school and was a revelation, since my school up until then didn't include any kind of organized or regular music. What completely fascinated me was the quality of music kids just like me could produce. Well, maybe they weren't just like me; they, after all, had kept up their music lessons. I was especially impressed by the staged musicals and their ability to draw me so completely into the emotional and situational reality of their story. *Oklahoma* and *Guys & Dolls* were my favorites. I would dearly have loved to have been a major player in one of our musicals in high school, but I'm afraid I was too busy trying (without a whole lot of success) to be "popular." The closest I got to stardom was to take out the girl who played Nancy in *Guys and Dolls*, and even that was before she was in the play.

The school I attended first through eighth grade had no music program, either performance or appreciation. The one exception, however, proved to be notable to me. When I was in sixth grade, the new eighth-grade teacher, Miss Poniatowski (when we were in eighth grade, we called her "Pony, but *not* in her hearing), came around a few times to play recorded classical music. She must have convinced the nuns that we needed some culture. Whereas that was unquestionably true, apparently we got enough culture awfully quickly, because our musical education didn't last long, only a few sessions.

The only piece of music I remember from this brief music appreciation experience is the *William Tell Overture.* This doubtless was because I was a big fan of the Lone Ranger, and what kid at that time didn't thrill to that heroic gallop of music as the masked man rode thundering off with a cloud of dust and a hearty "Hi O, Silver"? I have always remembered sharing this experience with Miss P., because it was fascinating to me that this powerful musical theme came from and fit into a much larger piece of music. It was equally intriguing that this music without words told a heroic story, as explained by Miss P., that tied in so well with the TV program.

When I was in college, I did finally develop a deep appreciation for classical music, aided by the fact that my school, Oakland University, hosted the Meadowbrook Music Festival, the summer home of the Detroit Symphony Orchestra. Students, then, could get into concerts free, to spread their blankets on the grassy hillside and listen, under the stars, as the sumptuous sound of Tchaikovsky and Copland and Rachmaninoff enveloped them from below. My wife and I took full advantage of this, as well as other free concerts in the area. Some of the best were free programs the Detroit Symphony used to put on in the parks in the summer.

Many concerts and thirty-some years after sixth grade, my wife and I were at a concert at Meadowbrook. Before the start, we were people watching, when I saw someone who looked familiar sitting at a table on the snack pavilion. "Julie, see that woman over there, I think that's my eighth grade teacher. Omigod, that's got to be her [she had a very distinctive look]. I'm going to go talk to her."

I did, and I got a chance to be on the giving end of the gift that teachers just love to get. I got to show a former teacher that I understood and appreciated what she had been trying to get across to us kids years ago. I got to tell her how her influence changed my life. It was sweet, I'm sure, for both of us.

***

Here's an easy Jeopardy answer: The #1 TV show that launched the careers of the most popular singers and resulted in scads of #1 songs and top 40 hits. If you said, "What is *American Idol*," sorry. The correct question is: "What is *Arthur Godfrey's Talent Scouts*," the #1 show in the 1951-52 season. I was too young to be a contributing statistic that year, and it probably wouldn't have been too interesting on the 8-inch set we had. I certainly remember it later, though—it lasted until 1958—on the new 19-incher we eventually got. Julie's family watched it religiously. She even wrote Godfrey a fan letter and got an autographed picture in return. Me, I had my own picture of Godfrey. Because the show was sponsored by Lipton tea, I somehow got the idea that Godfrey was the silhouetted man on the Lipton tea box.

Arthur Godfrey's Talent Scouts had absolutely none of the pizzazz and high production values of *American Idol,* but it did have some pretty bad acts that would have fit seamlessly into the "weirdo weeks" of *Idol* auditions. The show had its own auditions, and the weirdest thing of all is that it turned down both the amateur Elvis and Buddy Holly to be on the show! It also, however, gave a stage to the likes of Pat Boone, Connie Francis, The Diamonds, Tony Bennett, Johnny Nash, Patsy Kline, and Steve Lawrence.

The relationship between music and TV worked the other way, too, with established recording and radio stars switching over to TV One of the most common genres of early TV was the musical variety show, and many of the singers who scored consistently with record sales ended up hosting their own show. Dinah Shore is one of many TV singers whom I'm sure many of us kids didn't realize had successful careers as big band singers before TV What I remember most about her show, which ran from 1956 to 1963, was the "See the U.S.A. in Your Chevrolet" theme song. My family did get to see some of the U.S.A. in a Chevrolet after my parents bought a new Chevy in 1958. Pretty effective advertising, I'd say.

The Dinah Shore song that sticks in my head is "Chantez, Chantez," from 1957. A big radio hit, it was one of the few things I can remember picking up on the little crystal radio I had. It's popularity was probably what caused me to watch the TV show. As a nine year-old boy, I was pretty much ignorant of Dinah's twenty straight top-ten songs in the 40's and her previous TV and radio work. Interestingly enough, I am much, much more familiar today with Dinah Shore's early music. One of the best things about the electronics revolution is that we are able to go back in time to pick up and explore the music that we were too young to appreciate when it was popular or that happened before we were even born.

Another show that I watched a lot was Perry Como's *Kraft Music Hall*. It would have been hard not to see Perry, since he was on TV from 1948 to 1993! What I remember most about this show was the "Letters, we get letters" feature. I was enticed into watching by the great performers, whom I knew from their own hit songs, who were guests and often sang duets with Perry. He also sang his own songs, which were popular hits in their own right. He was, actually, the first recording artist to have ten records that sold a million copies, and his songs were all over the radio.

One thing that always confused me, though, was how could Ray Charles, the soul singer, be the leader of the Ray Charles Singers, Perry Como's backup group on the show and on records? I thought, "Maybe Ray Charles used to be in a church choir or something." This was especially curious to me when I saw Ray Charles, the soul singer, on Perry Como's show as a guest, and he didn't seem to have anything to do with the singers. Eventually I discovered that there was *another* Ray Charles.

Another music variety show I watched, that had a big star for a host, was the Dean Martin Show. I watched this mostly, again, because I liked Dean Martin's popular songs, including his theme "Everybody Loves Somebody Sometime," which especially appealed to me because, it seemed, I *always* loved somebody. I also knew Dean Martin from the movies and was an early Martin & Lewis fan. It was Jerry Lewis's goofy antics that appealed to me, as a goofy kid, and I was sad at their breakup. Lewis's first solo movie, *The Delicate Delinquent* made it clear that the goofiness would go on. It also had a special musical tie in. If you've never seen it, check out Lewis's classic encounter with the theramin, an instrument as wild as Lewis himself.

Dean Martin's personality and character onstage were just the opposite of Perry Como's. Como was soft spoken and gentle, a genuine Mr. Nice Guy, a TV role model that would be acceptable or better to just about any mother in America. He often wore cardigan sweaters (Hey, where do you think Mr. Rogers got it from?). Martin, on the other hand, always had a cigarette in his hand, regularly acted as if he were drunk (if, indeed he wasn't), and frequently talked and joked about drinking. He was a poster boy for Hollywood decadence. Thinking back, I am surprised that my parents never prohibited me from watching Martin. I guess it was because alcohol was (and is) the cheap and easily obtained drug of choice and drunkenness was generally treated as a big joke.

Not only did singers come off of records and slip into TV, television stars went the other way, too. Some of them literally grew into it. When Ricky Nelson scored his first single hit "I'm Walkin'," it coincided with his forming a band on *The Adventures of Ozzie and Harriet* TV show, on which he grew up playing the son of (his real parents) Ozzie and Harriet Nelson. After "Walkin'," he subsequently would play his latest song release at the end of most of the show's episodes--an early music video and a brilliant promotional technique. It became the part of the show that I and bazillions of other teens and pre-teens waited for.

In no other show that I can remember, did the transition from TV to music work out quite so seamlessly, but *The Donna Reed Show* did yield hits for Shelley Fabares ("Johnny Angel") and Paul Petersen ("My Dad"). I adored "Johnny Angel," as I did Shelley Fabares. As Mary, the big sister on the show, she had about the same age relationship to Pedersen as brother Jeff, as I did with my older sister. Petersen was also a veteran of the *Mickey Mouse Club* and not the only Mousketeer to score with records, either. The show's heartthrob, Annette Funicello, scored big with her paean to Paul Anka, "Tall Paul," and dozens and dozens of songs from her beach party movies.

Other stars on some of the shows I liked had their own hit records. Some of them tied in with their shows, like "Kookie, Kookie, Lend Me Your Comb," Edd Byrnes's spinoff from his role on "77 Sunset Strip." Others simply played on notoriety from the TV show. Gale Storm , *My*

Little Margie, had a big hit with "I Hear You Knocking" and several other top-ten records. Walter Brennan's "Old Rivers," and Lorne Greene's "Ringo," had nothing to do with their TV shows *The Real McCoys* and *Bonanza,* respectively, but both were successful spoken-word records.

One of the routines I remember well from *My Little Margie* was good-hearted, but meddlesome Margie being determined to find out who "Todd" was, from the firm of Honeywell & Todd, where her father worked. (Mr. Honeywell appeared in the series occasionally, but we never saw Todd.) Margie goes down to her father's office and encounters an old guy in the hallway who tells her he's "tahd" (tired). She, of course, mistakes him for Mr. Todd, and the usual madcap series of events ensues. This play on words has stuck in my head for more than fifty years, and surely contributed to my being an unrepentant punster. Parents and grandparents take note; be discriminating in what your kids watch; influences from TV can last a long, long time.

Some shows had such great musical themes that they became musical standards in themselves. *Bonanza* comes to mind, as does *Hawaii Five-O, The Beverly Hillbillies,* and *The Monkeys.* The theme from *I Love Lucy* was made into a disco version that got a lot of airplay in the 80's. Many of the shows' theme songs were actually pretty bland, though most of them were remarkably appropriate in feeling for the shows they introduced, including blandness! Some of them were quite distinctive and memorable as were their shows. How many of the themes from these shows can you whistle, starting with one that's made for whistling: *The Andy Griffith Show*: *The Dick VanDyke Show, Dragnet, Highway Patrol, Howdy Doody Time, Leave It To Beaver, Perry Mason, Make Room For Daddy, My Three Sons?*

***

Almost since the beginning of commercial TV, there have been music shows that were dedicated to various genres of music. Beginning in the early 50's, TV viewers could find classical orchestral music (including the New York Philharmonic and the NBC Symphony), opera, jazz, folk music, and country music broadcasts. In the later 1950's rock and roll dance party shows started popping up in local markets all over the country. In Philadelphia, in 1952, Bob Horne's Bandstand began broadcasting the movin' and groovin' of Philly teens. The show's host was changed to a fresh-faced 26 year-old named Dick Clark in 1956. On August 5, 1957, the show went national on ABC, and *American Bandstand,* arguably the best teen music show ever, was born.

I have to admit that I wasn't exactly a fan for a while. *Bandstand* was on just before the *Mickey Mouse Club*, and for a short time was on both *before and after* the Mouse. With all the things there were to do, it was hard to make time for both shows. Plus, by the time *Bandstand* started on national TV, the *Mickey Mouse Club* had been on for almost two years and had a tremendously loyal fan base, myself included. Everything about the *Mickey Mouse Club (especially Annette and Cheryl!)* appealed to me way more than anything about *American Bandstand,* so the Mouse had priority. The music was even great, and there was a lot of it. The Mouseketeers were always singing and dancing, and the musical guests were always kids.

Watching these kids do their thing every day was awe inspiring to me and has left me never doubting that with a little guidance kids can do just about anything they set their minds to. Some of the music was literally memorable. Who could forget Cubby O'Brien whaling on his drums! Can you *sing* "e-n-c-y-c-l-o-p-e-d-i-a"? You might be forgiven if you can't remember the words to at least one verse of the song Spin and Marty sang around the campfire at the Triple A Ranch, but you really ought to know the chorus (hint: it starts with "Jingle, jangle").

The Mickey Mouse Club started on October 3, 1955, and was on for an hour each day, through 1957. After that, it switched to a half hour. This was a near tragedy for me, and I blamed *American Bandstand* and those darned teenagers, at least in part. I did inevitably became a *Bandstand* fan. I secretly wanted to learn to do all those cool dances (I still do!), but it was way too embarrassing to let this be known to my family, especially my older sister, by practicing in front of the TV And, who would I dance with, one of my sisters? I would have rather used a wooden a chair as Elvis recommended in "Jailhouse Rock." I have always envied the guys who had a steady girl, with whom they could watch *Bandstand* and get good at all those dances. I also often wondered: Did the great dancing come because of the girlfriend, or did the girlfriend come because of the dancing? I would never find out from personal experience.

***

Just as I believe my generation has been profoundly influenced by television in forming our view of human nature, ourselves, and our expectations of life, I think television played and plays a significant role in how we understand and appreciate music. Nowhere are these twin influences more pervasive than in the theme songs and the accompanying music for series shows. If the characters and content of TV shows helps form our sense of life, its music is the music of life. It's no wonder, then, that children today can't do anything without "their music." For better or worse, we've passed on to them the notion that life is only real if it has a musical background. The creators and manufacturers of the electronic marvel of the moment have been endlessly resourceful in providing it.

Who are the people in your neighborhood,
the people who you see each day?

The Muppets

CHAPTER EIGHTEEN

Also Starring…

I would be remiss if I didn't say a bit more about my father and mother and the influence they had on me, because in many ways, they and their influence were typical of the boom times we lived in. I've already said a few things about my father, and there's not too much more to say about him, in my youth, besides that he worked a lot.

Working a lot, for fathers in those days, was both a matter of survival and a means to get ahead—at least a little. Fathers were the principle and often a family's only bread winner. If a wife or mother worked, it was generally part time and for far less money, even if it was the same job as a man's. This meant that a man often needed to work as many hours as he could to make ends meet, or even take a second job or work on the side to provide a cushion or to buy *luxuries* such as a new car or television set. There were also serial recessions in the 50's that left many people intermittently out of work. I saw more than a few big tins of peanut butter or blocks of cheese marked with "USDA" in homes in my neighborhood.

This situation left women as sovereigns over the household most of the time, but as with other kids' mothers, it was implicit that my father was the ultimate authority. My mother exercised her own authority gently and primarily through high expectations. It was clear, though, that my father would apply the discipline if necessary, and then to back up my mother's interpretation of a situation.

I do remember roughhousing with my dad in a way I never would have imagined with my mother, and my mom would never have taken me fishing, as my dad did occasionally. I can also remember riding on my dad's back with my legs around him, as he swan under water on the few occasions he came down to the lake. These things stand out because they were relatively rare.

Just as he was available to do special projects for the neighborhood, my father made time to mow the little league field and to make and paint a large scoreboard to hang "runs" on—no electronics in those days. He came to my games, but he didn't often have time to play ball with us. He constructed a giant swing set for us, but we were on our own to use it. He did much of the remodeling of and adding on to our house himself, built the massive picnic table between two trees, and a executed a host of other special projects, but didn't always get to enjoy them as he should have.

For the most part, parents simply didn't play with their kids. The way I think most kids saw this was as a matter of freedom. We were pretty much left to do our own thing, and I have to say in my neighborhood, kids used their freedom responsibly, if not creatively. This freedom was, in part, a product of a lack of anxiety over child molesters and such, but also was a result of parents' believing that kids had a right to be kids without parental dictation.

I don't think my mother ever possessed a copy of Dr. Spock's *Baby and Child Care*, the parents' bible of the time, but her child-rearing role reflected his laissez-faire philosophy. She relied primarily on character building rather than rules, and she trusted the schools to do their job. She also expected and trusted us kids to exercise common sense. This was a far more reasonable expectation before the coming proliferation of radical and often self-destructive ideas and behaviors, and the media that carried them to kids. My mother was a woman of faith, but her faith was primarily in the inherent goodness of her children and our ability to use our heads.

Both my father and mother were in a class by themselves. Economically, our neighborhood ran from barely lower class to barely upper-middle class, with everything in between. The same held true, but even more so, for the parish we belonged to and the school it operated. My parents came from modest circumstances and worked hard at staying above the lower-class line, but they identified more with and aspired to become firmly upper middle class. This may not seem particularly significant, but it definitely reflects the increasing well-being of increasing numbers of people during these years.

My dad was invited to become partners with his boss when I was about eight. He borrowed the $10,000 to do so (a huge sum in those days) from my mother's older sister, my Aunt Jane's husband, my Uncle Jim. My dad worked his way into becoming "the boss," but he would never have even thought to have joined his "men" and their wives in the bar on Friday nights. My mother never once articulated it, but her subtle attitude made my sisters and me aware that we were a cut above. There was little pretension to this, and it was separate from the self-righteousness of being Catholic. There *was* a moral component, but my mother was raised Protestant, and her lessons were based much more on the Golden Rule and common decency than any doctrine. Her expectations were more along the lines that we would always be respectful, never get in trouble, always tell the truth, and never hurt someone else. We were also expected to read a lot, get A's and B's in school, take Latin, and go to college. These things were never pushed on us, but our path in life was never a question for us.

***

Aunt Kate and Uncle Ernie weren't really my aunt and uncle, but they *were* two of the realest people I've ever known. Kate was my Uncle John's sister, so there was a connection. Another connection is that they all had moved to our neighborhood in Michigan from Miamisburg, Ohio, just as my parents had.

Kate and Ernie were the kind of people a kid would choose for aunt and uncle if those positions were elective. Kate was an in-charge, competent person. She was also gentle and unassuming, so her authority grew from her knowing what to do and her willingness to do it. A kid could feel confident in her presence. What extended that feeling was her kindness and compassion. Ernie was the same way. He was "uncle" and friend to a lot of kids in the neighborhood, some of whom sorely needed that steady older influence. He was a talented carpenter, so their house was substantially the product of his handiwork, but his continuing province was outside the house. He was the champion mushroom hunter in the neighborhood and one of the very best game hunters and fishermen.

He and my Uncle John were the neighborhood turtle hunters. Why turtles? If you ever had pan fried turtle, you wouldn't have to ask. Their hunting technique was simple: walk in creeks and feel along under the banks for turtle holes, stick a hand in, and try to pull out a turtle. We're talking 20 to 30 pound alligator snappers! Their theory was that the turtle always went in head first, so the first thing their hand encountered would be its tail. This made a convenient handle to pull the turtle from its hole.

Apparently it worked, because they got a lot of turtles and never lost so much as a finger. My dad almost did, though. He and I went on a couple of turtle hunts with Uncle Ernie and Uncle John.

On one hunt, Dad pulled a turtle out of its hole, but it managed to get away. In trying to catch it mid-stream, he encountered what definitely was not the *tail* end, and almost lost the end of his finger. It definitely was safer to put your hand into the hole. On these two hunts, I got to carry the gunny sack with caught turtles. I learned pretty quickly, from being nipped on the back of my thigh, not to carry the sack slung over my shoulder, but to let it float in the water.

***

Kate and Ernie were also a love story. Kate had been an aspiring opera singer as a girl, but she chose to give it up for Ernie, a family, and a trip to Michigan. To me growing up, they presented (along with my own parents) the model of a stable, respectful, loving marriage. To the time Uncle Ernie died (a week ago as I write this), he and Aunt Kate were clearly very much in love (and married for sixty years). In the stability of their relationship, they were the rule for the neighborhood. Divorce was the exception, though there were a few women whose husbands were inexplicably (to me) absent. Apparently, running off was not necessarily cause for divorce.

One thing that sticks in my memory is that Aunt Kate would give homemade popcorn balls to my sisters and me trick-or-treating on Halloween. Since their house was at the opposite corner of the neighborhood from ours, it was a long walk, but it was worth it, not just for the popcorn balls, but to bask in Aunt Kate's kindness and "startled" appreciation for our costumes.

Though Kate and Ernie's house was a haven, on Halloween it wasn't from fear. Even the other kids' mostly homemade costumes were far from frightening. The miles-long trek through the neighborhood might have been a little scary, but it wasn't because there were no streetlights. We kids played outside in the dark a lot. It also wasn't because no adult accompanied us. We knew the "walking" neighborhood better than any adult did. It certainly wasn't because we worried someone might give us a "bad" treat, except for maybe *another* roll of Smarties. By the time we got to Aunt Kate and Uncle Ernie's house, we had walked a long way, we might have been rained or snowed on, we may have stepped in a mud puddle in the dark, and our costumes may have begun disassembling. A chance to sit down for a bit in a warm house and have a cup of hot chocolate was just the ticket.

***

My Aunt Phyllis and Uncle John lived only a few blocks from us and had moved from Ohio at the same time as my parents. If my Uncle John was gruff and snarly, my Aunt Phyllis was empathetic and bright. That isn't to say she was a shrinking violet. She and Uncle John would disagree almost continuously. He would growl his opinion, ending with an emphatic "Phyllis!" And she would offer hers, often as a question, in a soft spoken but persuasive way, beginning with "Oh, John..." I'm not sure they ever convinced each other of anything, but I think any bystander would have taken Aunt Phyllis's side every time.

Aunt Phyllis was pretty and petite, the kind of small-town girl that every small-town guy would love to love. That's why Uncle John had a heart with "Phyllis" tattooed on one forearm. The tattoo would last until he died, and so would his love for the girl he married. They were one of the vast majority of couples in my world who clearly took the "'Till death do us part" of love and marriage seriously.

If Aunt Kate was mother to neighborhood kids, Aunt Phyllis was big sister. Like a big sister, she was someone they could confide in, a good listener. Also like a big sister, her assessments of their problems or circumstances wasn't sugar coated nor was her advice always what they wanted to hear. It was, however, always understanding and sincere, and *that* was what they wanted to hear. One of the jobs she had over the years was waitressing at Frank's Grill, across from West Bloomfield High School. It was a savvy hire by the grill's owner. I know I liked to go in there when she was working, and I'm sure a lot of other kids did too.

***

At the top of the Big Hill, in a log house stained the color of dark chocolate, lived Bill and Winnie Smith, who functioned as sort of surrogate neighborhood grandparents. Bill was retired, wore wire-rimmed glasses, and was bald on top with a white fringe combed straight down the sides of his head. His voice was high and a little bit gravelly, and the way he spoke was a bit blustery. A pipe grew from his mouth or hand pretty much all the time, and the air inside the house was thick with its incense. It's already gloomy interior was filled with dark, overstuffed furniture. There were knickknacks, decorative plates, pictures, and wall hangings everywhere, and the effect was a little spooky. In fact, I always connected that house with Hansel and Gretel, somehow.

Relieving this dark air was gray-haired Winnie, who looked and talked much like a thinner Aunt Bea. She was so nice and so grandmother like.

But weren't witches sometimes like that....hmmm? Because the Smith's house was between mine and the beach and most everywhere else out of the neighborhood, I'd go by it frequently. Bill was often outside and he would greet me or us, and Winnie would come out and invite us in for a cookie. The cookies were always ginger snaps, which I didn't especially care for. Still, I would go inside now and then.

I probably would have declined all of the Smith's invitations to come in and visit and maybe even would have gone out of my way to avoid going by their house, except that my mother told me that they were very nice people, and I needed to be nice back to them. I considered this a little odd, since my parents didn't appear to know the Smiths very well and didn't deliberately associate with them. There may have been something else behind this—as far as I know the Smiths had no children.

Years later, I thought about it and decided that their "strangeness" was only that they were of a different generation from me even my parents. They did things a little differently from what I was used to in my tiny bit of experience, kind of like my own grandparents at times. I'm grateful to my mother for the lesson I learned from this and for the opportunity to have brought a little happiness to some older people simply by virtue of being a kid. When I returned to the neighborhood after an absence of many years, I decided to stop in to see the Smiths, but they were gone.

I'm sorry, so sorry
Please accept my apology

Brenda Lee

CHAPTER NINETEEN

…and a few regrets

I was born with badly crossed eyes. By the time I was two, I had had two operations to shorten the muscles that control eye position and movement. I have worn glasses since I was two, and one of my eyes still moves to the inside when I look up. Forty years later, I learned that my eyes also focus separately; I can't focus in on something with both eyes at once. These things profoundly influenced me, growing up, especially my self-confidence. I was called "four eyes" by other kids more times than I could possibly remember.

I played right field on my Little League team, the position of choice to put the least competent fielder. One time at practice, the assistant coach was hitting pop flys to us outfielders. I camped under one, determined to catch it. "I got it! I got it!" I got it all right, right in the crotch. The pain to my ego was far less intense than the pain to my body, but it lasted a lot longer.

I learned, from personal experience, that some kids would turn their own focus on any real or perceived weakness and pick at it. I learned as well, much to my chagrin, also from personal experience, that those who are low on the totem pole will often turn on someone who is even lower. This "totem pole" effect is something I went out of my way to point out to my middle school students. I taught academically and intellectually gifted middle school students, and it was very interesting to me that when

143

I assigned them to make a chart of the "social hierarchy" (a.k.a. "totem pole") for the school, they put themselves (A.I.G. students) at or near the bottom. The only group that regularly showed up on their charts as bigger social outcasts was special-education students. Being different in school, even if it's in some way being better, usually is a serious deterrent to popularity.

As a kid myself, popularity was my number one object of study. The time I spent pursuing it was enough to earn me about a "B minus" in the subject. It was also enough to cause my schoolwork performance to sink to about the same level. Had I devoted more of my time in school to school subjects, I have no doubt I would have been among the "smart" kids. There also is no doubt I would not have been among the "popular" kids. Smart was not in. Being or acting excessively dumb wasn't exactly an advantage either, but it was often more readily overcome than being "excessively" smart. Popular kids were, most often, in the academic middle class. Their relative disinterest in school allowed them time to pursue the sorts of things that would make them like the other popular kids. There were certain qualities necessary, of course; not everyone could be popular simply by trying. But, who defined what those qualities were?

What qualities made a kid cool and which ones made a kid an untouchable was always a mystery to me. I wonder now whether and how much the kids who were popular then knew *why* they were popular. I also wonder whether and how much the unpopular kids *cared* that they were. The kids who were not popular because they were too smart or, in my parochial school too pious, probably didn't care at all. I hope the others, who were unpopular because they were shy or physically less attractive, didn't care much either, because if they cared as much as I did, they were miserable. I really have no clue which it was because, admittedly, at this period in my life, I had little empathy for those "below" me.

***

During my childhood, the people who were, in my all-white world, lowest on the totem pole were African Americans. One incident relating to my Little League team calls this to mind. I have a fairly broad nose. One of the best players on the team used to call me "niger nose." He pronounced it just like the country Niger, but his meaning was clear. I would like to say that I beat the crap out of him in the name of racial justice, or at least nailed him with a snappy comeback. I pretended, however, that I didn't know what he meant. I hadn't been to Oz yet.

I grew up, into college, with absolutely zero personal contact with

African Americans. I can't say I was particularly prejudiced, but I was extremely ignorant--at least as ignorant as the media appeared to be and the opinions of those around me were. Given the effective segregation of the times, I am sure I share this circumstance with a great majority of my generation. What a shame.

Aside from seeing black people on the street when I would occasionally go to Pontiac with my parents, my principle exposure was through the *Amos and Andy* TV series. Years later, I used to listen with my own children to old-time radio programs on a Detroit station on Sunday nights. At Christmas time, the station presented a whole evening of Christmas programs from different radio shows. The one from *Amos and Andy*, played on radio by white men, was wonderful, with a very thoughtful lesson. I had developed a friendship with a black man, about thirty years older than I. I mentioned this radio program to him in a positive light once, and he was quite offended that I presented the program in a positive light. It didn't affect our friendship, but I did learn a lesson.

Since moving to North Carolina, I interact closely with African Americans every day. My African-American middle school students seemed to me woefully ignorant of the struggle that won their civil rights and how very recently the schools were legally segregated. Or, maybe it's just that they don't want to acknowledge what happened to their parents and grandparents. It is awfully humiliating for all of us. There definitely has been an enormous change for the better, but we cannot afford to forget how things used to be. This is especially true since the change to an integrated society is far from being completed even yet.

***

There was a young man in my neighborhood, named Ivo, who was "deaf and dumb." I would only see Ivo maybe three or four times a year, quite by chance. For whatever reason, he stayed inside almost all the time and only went on occasional walks.

Ivo was probably in his twenties. He had short dark hair and large dark eyes. He was a bit overweight, and it seemed that every time I saw him he had on the same clothes, baggy khaki pants and a light blue-green and cream plaid sport shirt. Whenever I got close to Ivo, he would smile and make happy, wordless sounds that clearly were meant to convey good feelings. I was afraid of him. He was abnormal, and abnormal in the 50's was scary. It was also something most people chose to keep behind closed doors.

I recalled the story of Ivo to my eighth grade students the first time I had my class read *To Kill A Mockingbird*. There were striking parallels with Boo Radley, except that Ivo, so far as I knew, never did anything "crazier" than not being able to hear or speak. When I think of it, my reluctance to interact with Ivo is one of the regrets of my life. It was born of ignorance, so I don't feel guilty. But what if I had deliberately been nice to him, and tried to get to know him?.

I don't know how I knew it, but Ivo was supposed to be a mathematical genius. What if he *was* a mathematical genius? Maybe we could have "talked" about numbers. Maybe he could have helped me to overcome one of my other regrets in life, also born of ignorance; maybe I could have gotten *good* at math.

But more, much more than this
I did it my way.

Frank Sinatra

CHAPTER TWENTY

From dust ye came…

My sainted mother could have attested to the genesis of dust. We lived on dirt roads, and I always brought some dust home with me, whether it was ground into my previously white tee shirt or a fog on my previously shiny school shoes. Our dust was fine and gritty at the same time. A car would pass, and the sandy grit would quickly settle out from the cloud that would linger and slowly fall. Sooner or later another car would pass, and it would start all over again. It was a cycle. It was a way of life. It is life.

I've been back to the old neighborhood a few times over the years, the last time only a few years ago. I hardly recognized any of the places that had been the stage for the early acts in my life's play. The bumpy, dusty dirt roads were all paved. The break with the past was all so clear and clean; still, I brought a little dust with me. The vacant lots that once were little parks in themselves, for building forts or camping out or picking gallons of blackberries, were all now yards with houses. The big woods had turned into the wooded lots of the huge, expensive houses in the development that built across from the other side. The Club House had long ago burned down, and the expansive beach of my memory had shrunk as my world had grown. The "big raft," that had taken me years, as a child, to get up the courage and develop the skill to swim out to, was actually not much more than a good stone's throw away.

The lake was smaller than I remembered, but it doesn't matter. One of my favorite books as I was growing up was *McElligott's Pool*, by Dr. Seuss. If you're not familiar with it, *McElligott's Pool* recounts the story of Mario, who goes to great length to explain to a scoffer why he is not such a fool for fishing in a diminutive water hole. He imagines every sort of amazing fish that he *might* catch, how the water hole *might* be connected by an underground stream to the very ocean! The book had a profound influence on my life, both philosophically and practically. It caused me, as a kid, to want to explore every body of water bigger than a bathtub in anticipation of what *might* be in it. It also caused me to look below the surface of people, things, and ideas. It caused me, for better or worse, to sit for endless hours on my lake with a cane pole in my hands, waiting to catch a BIG one. I haven't caught it...yet. It's still there waiting for me, though, for anybody.

There was a song sometime back: "All We Are Is Dust in the Wind." Maybe that's some of what we are, but it makes it that much easier for our lives to touch each other and sometimes to combine. Case in point: I am reasonably certain that I was the very best tree climber in the neighborhood. It's a distinction I enjoyed, like being the best berry picker, pretty much by default, since to my knowledge no one else was particularly interested in pursuing either. Both ended up being solitary and self-motivated activities. They go along with other strands in my life, such as running cross country and wrestling in high school, majoring in Philosophy in college, and writing. Tree climbing had a mixed beginning, however, that goes back before I can even remember. There was a natural proclivity expressed in climbing up onto my neighbor's roof when I was two, but there was another incident that might have daunted someone less a product of evolution.

When I was quite young, before my little sister was born, a neighbor boy would occasionally baby sit for my older sister and me. One day when he was watching us, we all went outside and walked down the road a bit. In the little woodsy lot beyond the house next door, little monkey that I was, I began climbing a small tree. I can't attest to the rest of this scenario, because I can't be sure if I actually remember it or have only heard the story so many times that it *seems* that I remember it. At any rate, I fell out of the tree from about twelve feet up, and the babysitter, Jim (not my pal Jim, who didn't move in until four or five years later) *caught* me.

My sister, who was five at the time, attests to this, as does Jim. The only reason that I have to be skeptical is that this would be the *only* time I have *ever* fallen out of a tree, and it seriously compromises my record as a tree climber. Otherwise, I have pretty good reason to believe the story is true. Jim went off not long after this to the seminary to become a priest. His family moved away after a few years, and my family pretty much lost touch of what Jim was doing. A dozen years or so after the ignominious tree incident, when my family finally moved from the neighborhood, who should be the assistant pastor in our new church but Father Jim.

This was also the church of my wife-to-be, whom I met for the first time that summer through the church teen club. Despite a fun summer, in which we won a golf tournament together and went down the Detroit River on a big cruise boat to the amusement park on Bob-Lo Island, we didn't associate much for the next two years of high school.

After our freshman year at different colleges, we began dating again, and decided, at nineteen, to get married. Though we both had serious doubt about our faith, we decided that we *had* to get married by Father Jim. It was a decision that made both of our parents very happy. I'm not sure if it made me happy or not; I was already so ecstatic to be marrying the girl of my dreams that I couldn't have told how I felt about the *ceremony* (yeah, I know, just like a *guy*). We had a small ceremony, and don't you know, my best buddy Ron was best man.

I heard someone on the radio a while back criticizing wedding vows' "till death do us part" as putting totally unrealistic expectations upon young married couples today. All I know is that when I got married for life, it was that *expectation*, in part, that has helped to make the commitment a reality for 43 years so far. Maybe it's time we dusted off and defended some of the old principles we learned to live by as kids.

***

I'm a great believer in the physical, mental, and spiritual value of play for children. I also believe that the majority of play should be outside. How in the world do we expect kids to understand and respect Nature if they don't experience it as a normal, everyday part of their play? I spent a week with four generations of my wife's family on aptly named Grand Lake, in Northern Michigan, some years after the aforementioned backyard wedding reception. One of those grand nephews who had played himself out at that wedding spent almost every waking minute of that week mesmerized by a hand-held video game, much of the time sitting on a picnic table at the edge of the lake.

Presumably this wasn't normal behavior for him—he had spent his life to this point living in Northern Michigan, after all. But it made me think of *modern* kids, who reportedly, at least, deliberately spend as much time as possible indoors. The digital revolution is, in part, the cause. Kids spend an inordinate amount of their time attached to electronic devices. Most of these have become quite portable enough to be used outside, but what's the point. A kid focused on a game or texting friends is focused on that. A young person talking on a phone outside is almost surely in transit to some place indoors. We had our TV's as well, and our transistor radios, but they were so much less overwhelming.

Another reason kids might be stuck inside is parental fear of the sun. The sun! Of course, it's common sense to avoid sunburn, and a family history of melanoma has to be taken seriously. But the latest scientific evidence is that we aren't getting *enough* sun, and that's much more dangerous than getting a reasonable amount. *All good things in moderation.* Geez, Aristotle was teaching that twenty four hundred years ago.

A moderate amount of sun and a moderate amount of dust never hurt anyone. That's the kind of wisdom we Boomers can and ought to draw from a reasonable consideration of our growing up. Things have changed much since then, and the pace of change promises only to accelerate. As we enter the time of our lives when wisdom is supposed to finally come to us, let us share that wisdom with those who take over making history from us. We can gently remind them, to paraphrase George Santayana, that those who are ignorant of the mistakes of the past are doomed to repeat them. At least as important for them to know, however, is that those who are ignorant of the simplicity, the freedom, and the sense of wonder of the past, they are doomed to *not* repeat them.

www.ingramcontent.com/pod-product-compliance
Lightning Source LLC
Chambersburg PA
CBHW020432290526
45785CB00002B/819